Women, HIV, and the Church

Women, HIV,
and the Church

In Search of Refuge

EDITED BY

Arthur J. Ammann

with

Julie Ponsford Holland

CASCADE *Books* • Eugene, Oregon

Cascade Books
An Imprint of Wipf and Stock Publishers
199 W. 8th Ave., Suite 3
Eugene, OR 97401

www.wipfandstock.com

ISBN 13: 978-1-62032-278-9

Cataloging-in-Publication data:

Women, HIV, and the church / Edited by Arthur J. Ammann and Julie Ponsford
Holland.

xviii + 180 p.; 23 cm—Includes bibliographical ref.

ISBN 13: 978-1-62032-278-9

1. AIDS (Disease)—Religious aspects—Christianity. 2. HIV infections—Religious
aspects—Christianity. 3. Church and social problems. I. Ammann, Arthur J., 1936–. II.
Holland, Julie Ponsford. III. Title.

BV4460.7 W58 2012

Manufactured in the USA

This book is dedicated to women throughout the world—many of whom have shared their stories with us face to face—struggling with the consequences of HIV. With patience and courage, they hold to the hope that the Christian church will reach out to them and all those who suffer, no matter the cause. In honor of these brave women, we ask the Christian Church to become participants with God in providing a refuge for the suffering, especially for those with HIV.

The authors have generously agreed to donate their proceeds from the sale of this book to benefit women affected by violence in resource poor countries. Proceeds will be given to Global Strategies for HIV Prevention serving women around the world.

At one point in the interview, Martha said, "I asked God what he wanted me to do." We realized that, in spite of all the death and pain and suffering that she had experienced as a result of HIV, and in spite of all of the discrimination that she had witnessed and feared, Martha continued to derive her strength from God, who directed her life. She was alive, she felt, because God wanted her to minister to others. She would continue to go to church and worship and talk to God alone, who provided her with the love and understanding that she needed. There in church, she would be surrounded by people who might not understand how far God's love reaches. They would be the ones who would miss out on the blessing of providing a refuge for the sick and suffering.

We ended the interview by asking Martha, "With all that you experienced, all the pain and suffering that you endured, what would you like to do the most?"

Martha replied, "What I want to do is save people's lives. If I can save one or two, that is what I want to do."

— FROM AN INTERVIEW WITH A WOMAN WITH HIV IN THE U.S.

Contents

Contributors

Arthur J. Ammann, M.D. Founder of Global Strategies for HIV Prevention and advocate for HIV prevention and care for women and children. Clinical Professor of Pediatrics, University of California, San Francisco Medical Center. Dr. Ammann became engaged in the HIV epidemic when it was first discovered in 1981, and he has conducted research and directed programs for women and children in resource-poor countries on HIV prevention and care throughout the world. He has published numerous articles and essays on these subjects, and he has spoken on issues surrounding the injustices of HIV nationally and internationally. He is the co-editor (with Arye Rubinstein) of *Prevention and Treatment of HIV Infection in Infants and Children.*

Darrel W. Amundsen, Ph.D. Professor Emeritus of Classics at Western Washington University. He is the author of *Medicine, Society, and Faith in the Ancient and Medieval Worlds* and co-author with Edward J. Larson of *A Different Death: Euthanasia in the Christian Tradition,* and co-editor with Ronald L. Numbers of *Caring and Curing: Health and Medicine in the Western Religious Traditions.*

Daniel B. Clendenin, Ph.D. Founder of Journey with Jesus www.journey withjesus.net with a mission characterized by six values: biblical fidelity, cultural relevance, critical inquiry, pastoral sensitivity, global awareness, and ecumenical generosity. He is the author of *Many Gods, Many Lords: Christianity Encounters World Religions; Eastern Orthodox Christianity: A Western Perspective;* and five other books.

Sharon Gallagher, M.T.S. Editor of *Radix* magazine and associate director of New College Berkeley, where she teaches classes on "Women Empowered to Serve." She has recently edited *Where Faith Meets Culture: The* Radix *Magazine Anthology.*

Contributors

David W. Gill, Ph.D. Mockler-Phillips Professor of Workplace Theology & Business Ethics, Gordon-Conwell Theological Seminary, South Hamilton, Massachusetts. Author of *Doing Right: Practicing Ethical Principles* and six other books.

Mark A. Labberton, Ph.D. Lloyd John Ogilvie Institute of Preaching at Fuller Seminary, Director, Associate Professor of Preaching. His books include *The Dangerous Act of Worship: Living God's Call to Justice* and *The Dangerous Act of Loving Your Neighbor.*

Nyambura J. Njoroge, Ph.D. Minister, Presbyterian Church of East Africa (PCEA). She is Kenyan and holds a doctorate in Christian Social Ethics from Princeton Theological Seminary, and previously coordinated World Council of Churches' Program for Ecumenical Theological Education (ETE). She is currently in charge of WCC/Ecumenical HIV and AIDS Initiative in Africa (EHAIA).

Erika Nossokoff. International Coordinator for Faith Alive Foundation–Nigeria, a hospital in Jos, Nigeria, that provides medical and social services at no cost to the patients. The hospital is well-known for its Christian compassion and care for all individuals with HIV regardless of religious beliefs. She is the author of *Faith Alive: Stories of Hope and Healing from an African Doctor and His Hospital.*

Susan S. Phillips, Ph.D. Executive Director and Professor of Sociology and Christianity, New College Berkeley (an affiliate of Berkeley's Graduate Theological Union). Dr. Phillips, a sociologist and spiritual director, also regularly teaches Christian spirituality for Fuller Theological Seminary, Regent College, and San Francisco Theological Seminary. Her books include the award-winning *The Crisis of Care: Affirming and Restoring Caring Practices in the Helping Professions* (with Patricia Benner), and *Candlelight: Illuminating the Art of Spiritual Direction.*

Nupanga Weanzana, Th.D. President, Bangui Evangelical School of Theology (BEST), Bangui, Central African Republic. Dr. Nupanga Weanzana has served as the director of the theological school, as an Old Testament professor, as an author, and as a pastor at several different churches. He has also lived in multiple African countries, providing him with a wide understanding of culture and spirituality.

Preface

ARTHUR J. AMMANN

Why This Book, and Why Now?

IMMERSED IN THE GLOBAL HIV epidemic for over 30 years, I have observed the disproportionate impact of HIV on women and children. Of the number of people who are infected with HIV worldwide, the percentage of women has increased from 5% at the beginning of the epidemic to over 50% today. Additionally, because most of the women infected during the history of this epidemic have been of childbearing age, there has been a concomitant increase in the number of infants with HIV, as well as a secondary epidemic of orphaned children—those experiencing the loss of mothers who succumbed to the infection.

As I witnessed the HIV epidemic evolving, I fully anticipated that Christians would embrace those who were affected just as Jesus set the example by focusing on and embracing those who were sick and dying. After all, I had over my many years as a physician observed Christians and the Church as a whole respond to those with other diseases—praying with them, giving comfort, providing them with food, and embracing them and their families in their sorrow. But, as if the physical pain and suffering that HIV produces were not enough for the women with HIV, they were too often themselves blamed for having become infected. Too many who sought refuge in the churches they attended—churches where they had served the sick and the poor—were turned away as they now sought refuge for themselves and their children.

There is a need for a comprehensive book presenting sound theological and scientific principles for a Christian response to the HIV epidemic. Several books and essays have been written in the past by outstanding internationally recognized authors; yet many of us realize that discrimination and stigmatization of women continues, and that the Church has yet to play a major role in reversing many of these injustices. For the content represented here, we have called on individuals who have made contributions on these topics in the past and on new voices that can offer perspectives not yet considered. The focus of this book will be women, HIV, the Church, and the desperate need of these women for a refuge from their pain, suffering, and rejection, as well as the Christian theology that urges the Church to provide a refuge for all affected by the epidemic.

From the beginning, we the authors envisioned a book of essays authored by multiple individuals recognized and skilled in the presentation of the issues that are relevant to developing a sound theological response. The book is directed to college, university, and seminary students and faculty; university-oriented churches; church and lay leaders; and campus Christian groups who focus on issues affecting the international community and, especially, who desire to develop a ministry to engage and assist women with HIV.

A Personal Perspective

Having been engaged in the HIV epidemic for so long, I now have a better understanding of why so many of Christ's teachings concern the poor and suffering. As HIV has spread, I have seen firsthand the increasing needs of those who suffer from an incurable disease. In trying to understand my own spiritual response to the epidemic, I pored over the gospels. Answers were found in the words of Jesus, especially in John 4, which recorded his meeting with the Samaritan woman at the well. This woman was so important to him that he went out of his way to meet with her, even though many condemned her. Perhaps today this woman would have been infected with HIV.

Here, then, is one of the distinctive teachings of Jesus on how we as Christians are to respond to the HIV epidemic today: We are taught that, no matter what the cause of a person's pain and suffering, or what religion they follow, or to what gender they belong, we are to respond with the compassion and forgiveness that typified every aspect of Jesus's life.

The path to my understanding was further clarified following an invitation by a Christian Indian friend to speak in Chennai, India, at India's first international conference on HIV. In a way, I did not look forward to going, as I had heard so much about the severity of the poverty in India that I feared that I would return to the U.S. depressed and overwhelmed. I was asked to be the opening-ceremony speaker and to challenge the community to respond to HIV prevention. How could I bring any encouragement to this country of over a billion people? The injustices and indifferences of an entire health care system loomed before me. I, from a developed country, with the most advanced health care system in the world, was being asked to bring hope and encouragement to a nation of poverty.

On the morning of my talk, in my hotel room, I sat and read Matthew 8:1–4. Jesus reached out and healed the leper who came to him. There must have been thousands of lepers in Israel at that time, but he healed only one. I got up and looked out the window, and I saw the children entering the schoolyard, happy and eager even as they waded through the water and mud from a flooding rain the previous evening. They were but a few of the tens of millions of children in India, but each one was important. It was then that I understood what God asks of us. We are to reach out one by one—the leper, Nicodemus, the woman at the well, and the one with HIV. The message of hope begins with a single individual.

It was then that I also began to think more deeply about the role of Christians throughout the world in this HIV epidemic. Much blame has been placed on those who had no choice in whether or how they became infected. It seemed time for compassion to replace blame, as we read in John 9:1–3: "As he went along, he saw a man blind from birth. His disciples asked him, 'Rabbi, who sinned, this man or his parents, that he was born blind?' 'Neither this man nor his parents sinned,' said Jesus, 'but this happened so that the work of God might be displayed in his life.'" It was hard for me to escape the conclusion that God was leading me and others to respond with compassion to the millions of those suffering from HIV, to demonstrate his love for all.

As I continued speaking and visiting developing countries, I met many wonderful and compassionate Christians caring for those with HIV. Some of them were themselves infected. They were doing what they could with minimal resources. I would return to wealthy California and ask myself, couldn't we do more? Over and over again, I read the challenge of Jesus to help the poor and needy, and to care for the widows and orphans. With an epidemic that had produced over 16 million orphans, couldn't the Christian community do more? And couldn't the Christian community shout a clarion call to protect the vulnerable and to provide a refuge for those who suffer?

This book of essays was put together to provide not just an overview of the HIV epidemic as it affects women and their children, but also to present a theology of how we are to respond to those in need, no matter the cause of their suffering. This book also urges Christians always to be in the forefront of responding to those in need. It is a reminder to us all that, no matter what catastrophe may occur, even if we do not understand the "why"s, we can act.

As I read the words of John 4 time and again, they became an intimate guide as to how I should act with compassion and understanding in response to people who are suffering. The words are so relevant to a Christian response to the HIV epidemic today that I took the liberty of writing a contemporary interpretation, hoping and praying that the teachings of Jesus will always direct our actions toward those in desperate need of his love.

A Personal Interpretation of John 4:1–42

Jesus had been teaching all day. His followers, who were with him, realized how long they had traveled and that it was now noon—and they hadn't had anything to eat. Knowing their physical concerns, he let them to go in search of food while he rested by a fountain in the city square. (Jesus knew that, if his followers stayed, they would be offended because of the woman he was soon to meet, and that he was to share with her deep spiritual truths that he had not yet revealed to them.)

His followers had left to search for food, but they were reluctant to leave because of their secret concern about who Jesus might meet while he was alone, as they knew that the fountain was in an area where outcasts and prostitutes frequently gathered.

While Jesus was sitting on the edge of the fountain, a woman came to rest on the other side. It was for her that he had decided to travel through Samaria. Jesus knew all about her. He even knew that she had several sexual partners.

Jesus slowly turned toward her until they made eye contact.

"May I have a drink of water from your bottle?" Jesus asked. Startled, the woman replied, "You're asking me for a drink of water? You don't even know who I am. Besides, I've been drinking from this bottle all day, as have my friends. Aren't you afraid of catching something?"

"If you knew who I really am, you would ask me to give you living water to drink—water that would give you life beyond your dreams."

Puzzled, the woman said, "I don't understand what you mean. Are you a miracle worker, or are you trying to take advantage of me, just like every other man around here?"

Jesus replied, "Everyone who drinks the kind of water that you have in your hand will be thirsty again. There will be no end to your thirst. Every day, you will need to find more. But the water that I can give you is spiritual, and it can flow inside you to become a fountain of its own that will nurture you into everlasting life."

"You're trying to trick me," the woman said. "I've never heard anybody talk like that. But, I must admit, if what you're saying is true, at least it would be one part of my life that I wouldn't have to worry about. Tell me more about this living water so I won't ever be thirsty again. And if you have living food, tell me about that, too, so I won't ever be hungry again. And while you're at it, if you know anything about living medicines, tell me about that, too, so I won't ever have to take another pill for my HIV ever again."

Jesus did not answer her requests. Instead, he said, "Go to the other side of the park and bring your husband over here, so I can talk to him, too."

Frightened, she said, "I have no husband."

"You're right," Jesus replied. "You've had a lot of sexual partners, and the man living with you now is not your husband."

"You must be some sort of a spiritual leader," she replied. Quickly changing the subject, she put on her most "pious" voice and blurted out, "Some say that their teachings are correct, while others say that *their* teachings are correct. Who can you believe?"

Jesus responded, "There will be a time when these differences no longer exist. That time is now, for those who praise and pray to God in spirit and in truth. These are the kind of people that God is on the lookout for—people who are devoted to him and worship him in spirit and truth."

Deep emotions overwhelmed her. She had never experienced such feelings before with anyone. In a hushed voice she revealed to this stranger one of her deepest longings: "I know that there is a spiritual person called Christ, and when I meet him, he will recognize me and explain everything to me."

The moment arrived—the very reason why Jesus had gone to the fountain to seek out this one woman. Although his followers had been with him up to this point, it was not the time for them to be given the deep spiritual truths, nor would they understand the extent of God's love and forgiveness for this woman. Jesus approached her. He saw the woman's worn face and her frail body—too small, it seemed, to sustain a living person. He knew that she had once possessed a physical beauty that caused men to stop and stare and lust. But as he looked into her eyes, he saw what others had not seen: the beauty of her deep spiritual desire that had gone unfulfilled through all of her human relations. Jesus prayed quietly to his Father, "This is the woman. You sent me to seek her out and to entrust her with a spiritual teaching that will transform her life, and the lives of those around her. Her needs are great. She will listen, and she will understand and talk to others who are also in need. This is the woman whom men have abused—and when she lost her physical attraction, they discarded her like a piece of old clothing. She is the woman who teachers of religion said was not worthy to receive your Word. But you have never forgotten her."

Jesus said, "I am the one you have been looking for. I am the living water that will well up in you to bring eternal life."

No sooner had Jesus spoken these words than his followers reappeared. They were shocked to see him alone, talking to an outcast and obviously ill woman. "This will ruin his reputation as well as ours," one of them thought. "She might even be a prostitute and have HIV infection or something," another muttered. Still another thought, "I certainly hope he isn't talking to her about spiritual things without us." But none of them dared to openly express their thoughts to Jesus.

The woman turned and went to her friends. "You've got to meet someone I just talked to by the fountain—he knew everything I'd ever done! I wonder if this is the Christ we've sometimes heard about."

"If he is the Christ," they replied, "why haven't any of the religious leaders been here to tell us about him?" Suspicious, they nevertheless followed her and made their way back to the fountain, because she was one of them and they trusted her.

Meanwhile, Jesus's followers were urging him to eat. "You must be starving," they said. "We brought you a sandwich and a drink."

Jesus looked at his followers with compassion. They had so much to learn. He had let them go and search for food while he had revealed one of God's deepest truths to this woman. He knew that they would not yet understand that she was in much greater need of spiritual healing than others and that, because of her needs, she was more prepared than they to receive his truth. He also knew how little they understood about love and forgiveness and how it would prevent them from understanding spiritual truths. It seemed strange that this woman, and not they, would be the recipient of God's special spiritual teaching.

Once again, Jesus's followers urged him to eat. But Jesus said, "I don't need anything to eat right now. This woman, who now understands the truth of living water, has fed me spiritually. What she has been given she will share with others, so they, too, will not be hungry. It is to people such as these that my Father has asked me to speak, and, through obeying my Father, I have been fed abundantly."

By this time, many of the outcasts had arrived with the woman to meet Jesus for themselves. "This person isn't like anybody we've ever heard before," they said. "Now we believe for ourselves that he must be our Savior, and the Savior of the whole world."

Imagining Jesus and this group of outcasts congregating beside the well is a picture of encouragement to me. Perhaps we, as Jesus's followers, can pattern a similar approach in response to the epidemic of HIV. Jesus didn't ignore this woman in need, nor did he become overburdened by all that needed to be done; he simply went out of his way to meet her face to face, mirroring back the dignity and beauty that his Father had put there in the first place, offering living water as a solution to the pain and longing deep within her. It is my hope that, through this collection of essays, we will realize how vital it is to continue the process Jesus began there at the well, seeing in one woman all that God saw in her since the day she was conceived.

1

Women, HIV, and the Heart of God

MARK A. LABBERTON

THE OPEN WINDOWS AND stillness left the impression that the room I was entering was empty. As I stepped through the doorway, my eyes adjusted from the bright Rwandan sunshine to the darkness inside. The room was not only *not* empty—it was filled. I had entered at the rear of the room, and I saw before me the backs of 60 silent women, crowded onto backless benches, waiting. Rose, a local nurse, escorted me to the front of the room and introduced me. There I stood, looking into the blank, gaunt faces of a roomful of women infected with HIV. Each fearful and undone. Each spurned and isolated. Each fragile and persevering. Each known and loved by God.

That scene could be duplicated in tens of thousands of places around the world—and these would be the marginally better stories among the 40 million victims of the HIV/AIDS pandemic. In the room that day, mutual understanding and suffering created at least a modicum of community. Those women could talk with candor. They could weep, if they had the strength. They could see in one another's faces what they knew was in their own. They could get advice. They could find medical assistance. They could be reminded that they are not alone.

Again and again, HIV/AIDS exposes in exquisite, clarifying relief what is true of the world's worst crises: Women suffer most. That the gathering that day in Rwanda was almost exclusively women was not a disproportionate aberration of the affected population. Some men were present in the room, and certainly millions of men have suffered and died from the disease. But the biological pathology of HIV/AIDS matches its social pathology, and that means women bear the heaviest burden of all.

The challenges and consequences of this gender-weighted reality are devastating and manifold. They are felt in every life, family, village, town, or city where this plague has visited. For people of Christian conscience, however—people who follow the God whose heart bends towards "the widow and the orphan"—the rampaging implications of HIV/AIDS for women and children is virtually paradigmatic.

The vulnerability of women as victims of men inside and outside the community of faith fills many pages of the Bible, as well as the annals of history. The economic and social circumstances of many women around the world in the twenty-first century are little better than they were in the biblical times, as documented in worldwide statistics. One in five women worldwide will become a victim of rape or attempted rape in her lifetime.

Even in the U.S., with its multitude of laws designed to shield women from violence, it occurs at rates much higher than people think. The Justice Department estimates that one in five American women will also experience rape or attempted rape during her college years, and that less than 5 percent of these rapes will be reported. Over the last two years, nearly 800,000 women were victims of reported rape or sexual assault in the U.S. One in five American high school girls has been physically or sexually abused by a dating partner. Most notably, in the U.S. as well as in other places, the Church has been largely silent.

The general implications of these statistics are extensive, and the medical ones are even more pointed. The social factors that leave women so vulnerable, along with the speed and viciousness of HIV, have combined to make this disease virtually unparalleled in the causation of both needless suffering and untimely death of women.

The HIV/AIDS crisis screams out for a compassionate and sustained Christian response. But such a response has *and* has not been the case. The reasons are many.

To begin with, there is a failure to affirm the equality of persons that the Christian faith upholds. The biblical tradition affirms that each person is of equal dignity and worth to any other. Women and men bear the image of God. Gender, race, and status do not make or undermine the value of a human life. Though Genesis 2 has been used to scapegoat women for the human fall from Eden, this view would be an abuse of the text in which both the man and the woman are found guilty: Both are clothed by the God of grace, who also judges and sends them from the garden.

The stipulations of the covenant include honoring and protecting the well-being of women to a degree that is remarkable in its time. The constant theme in the Law of God acknowledging the dignity and the vulnerability of women and children underlines that Yahweh wants the covenant community to be a safe haven of respect for the bodies and lives of women. All the more so is this case for the widow, whose well-being should be one of the distinct preoccupations of the people of God. Some of the fiercest words of the prophets came down on Israel for its failure to live up to this divine expectation.

In New Testament terms, the ministry and teaching of Jesus honor and value women equally with men, and break through hierarchical barriers like race and class. The history of biblical interpretation and theological practice in the Christian tradition has often and tragically placed many—especially poor—women in diminished statuses and roles. This is the exact opposite of both the ministry of Jesus and the ministry of the apostles.

This painful story of theological and moral failure, especially towards poor women of color, is writ large in the HIV/AIDS crisis. Mapping the statistics of HIV against indicators of race, gender, and class will reveal how the rampage of the disease has taken advantage of all the ways nations and societies fail to treat people with equality. When this gross disparity demonstrates the bias of cultures, it is one thing. But it is surely more indicting when it also reflects the bias of the Church.

It is taken for granted that Church and culture exist in a complex, dynamic relation. No simplistic pattern exists in any nation. However, the HIV crisis exposes that the overarching inequities of class, race, and gender that mark the patterns of particular cultures, or of dominant global culture generally, are not challenged or opposed by Christian practices, but rather mirrored. The layers of disparity get piled on: Being a woman, being poor, being sexually "tainted," being pregnant—each layer adds a greater burden to millions who suffer from cultural and spiritual isolation, condemnation, and neglect.

The arch paradigm of this dynamic can be seen in a context like eastern Congo, in a town like Goma. Surrounded by tribal wars, genocidal killing, widespread rape and violence against women, and rampant incidences of fistula, Goma is a strong example of our worldwide failure to live out the equality of persons. Eastern Congo has been shaped by the East African

Revival, which, in the second half of the twentieth century, involved a very high rate of Christian conversions. But the evidence of new faith being translated into changed social relations has been tragically weak. This has been true when we think of the military or paramilitary, but it has also been true within the life of the Church: Clergy and church leaders are sometimes perpetrators of sexual abuse and have contributed to a culture that is still often far more protective of male abusers than of female victims. Noteworthy counterpoints to these circumstances exist, but in Goma the pervasiveness of the Church does not manifest itself as a pervasiveness of efforts to guard women in need of extensive and unyielding protection.

> Cited statistics highlight the given fact that sexual violence against women is not confined to parts of Africa. Strikingly, the HIV epidemic in women in the U.S. reflects some of the same characteristics as those surrounding the epidemic in Africa. In the U.S., women account for more than one in four new HIV/AIDS cases. Of these newly infected women, about two out of three are African-American. Most of these women got infected with HIV from having unprotected sex with a man—many of whom know they are infected or likely to be infected. AIDS is now the leading cause of death for African-American women ages 25–34. And African-American women are more than 21 times as likely to die from HIV/AIDS as non-Hispanic white women.

Inseparably paired with this failure of Christian conviction is the failure to practice the equality of persons. It is one thing to affirm the equality of persons, but it is another to uphold it in actual practice. To do so demands standing against so many different cultural mores around the world. It does not seem to be an overstatement that the failure to practice the equality of persons in relation to women and children is perhaps among the most common forms of human rights abuse.

These abuses are violations of practice at the personal, social, institutional, and governmental levels. Equality of persons is often an easy affirmation to make, but to live it means confronting layers of prejudice and practice. It means living differently in the home, in the classroom, in the office, in the court—as well as in the bedroom. That failure can be rationalized where there is little accountability and few implications for the man who typically has greater social and economic—and sometimes even religious—power.

> If you have any encouragement from being united with Christ, if any comfort from his love, if any fellowship with the Spirit, if any tenderness and compassion, then make my joy complete by being like-minded, having the same love, being one in spirit and purpose. Do nothing out of selfish ambition or vain conceit, but in humility consider others better than yourselves. Each of you should look not only to your own interests, but also to the interests of others. Your attitude should be the same as that of Christ Jesus: Who, being in very nature God, did not consider equality with God something to be grasped, but made himself nothing, taking the very nature of a servant, being made in human likeness. And being found in appearance as a man, he humbled himself and became obedient to death—even death on a cross! Therefore God exalted him to the highest place and gave him the name that is above every name, that at the name of Jesus every knee should bow, in heaven and on earth and under the earth, and every tongue confess that Jesus Christ is Lord, to the glory of God the Father. (Philippians 2:1–11)

From the standpoint of the Bible, this sort of abuse of power is one of the things that the gospel of Jesus Christ is meant to revise and alter. No text makes this point more tangible than Philippians 2:1–11 and the willingness of our Lord to lay down his prerogatives to power in order to love and save the world. We are called to "have the same mind among you that was in Christ Jesus." That courageous, counter-intuitive, self-sacrificing love is meant to be the pattern for why and how we are to love and serve one another. That is a central call for those who are in Christ—who came not just to "save" us eternally but to transform us by the renewing of our minds and hearts to reflect the God who made us and who now desires to remake us. When the Church only calls people to personal salvation without commensurate social (let alone political) practice, however, it means that the implications of God's work in Christ have been severed from the real world—in which such changed lives are essential to faithful Christian witness.

What Can Be Done?

Evident is a double failure: A personal salvation without fortifying internal transformation, and a chasm between Christ's purpose-filled work and everyday happenstance. This quandary is not universal, nor does it have to be accepted as inevitable or irreversible. It does mean admitting, as with any historic and chronic human distortion, that one should not be naïve about the deep presumptions of prejudice that make change difficult. In a world where issues of power are some of the most shaping but resistant issues facing us in families, tribes, villages, cities, or nations, we never come to the task of social change without ourselves being embedded in contexts that shape our perceptions, our words, and our capacity for action. Likewise, everyone we may engage has a history—if not a stake—in the status quo.

> But because of his great love for us, God, who is rich in mercy, made us alive with Christ even when we were dead in transgressions—it is by grace you have been saved. And God raised us up with Christ and seated us with him in the heavenly realms in Christ Jesus, in order that in the coming ages he might show the incomparable riches of his grace, expressed in his kindness to us in Christ Jesus. For it is by grace you have been saved, through faith—and this not from yourselves, it is the gift of God— not by works, so that no one can boast. For we are God's workmanship, created in Christ Jesus to do good works, which God prepared in advance for us to do. (Ephesians 2:4–10)

"But God . . ." is re-creating the story. God, who is "rich in mercy," wills a different world—one in which the equality of persons in essence and in practice is recognized and reflected in daily action. The life, teaching, and ministry of Jesus show us this "new creation." Those who seek to follow him are meant to imitate that vision and live in that way.

Start with the Personal

Steps in God's direction must begin with practical, daily, personal steps. Here are some suggestions for Christian leaders and disciples alike.

Begin with your own prayerful reflection regarding your attitudes and practices concerning the equality of persons, especially women and children, in your own life. Be as honest and candid as you can be about the things that expose your views at their most basic and unguarded, when issues of prejudice may be the most evident. Let this lead you to confession, prayer, and intercession.

If you are in Christian leadership or serving as a preacher, set aside a couple of hours to go through the same kind of exercise in relation to your congregation's life. You can do this alone or perhaps with a small group of other leaders. If your group includes women, make sure they are carefully heard. As concretely as you can, state what you really affirm and practice about the equality of persons, especially women. What issues seem to exist? How might they best be addressed?

As you think about women in your town or city, especially women who are at the margins because of poverty, abuse, drugs, or other reasons, what evidence is there that you or your congregation affirm their full dignity and value and make efforts to commit yourself to their care?

Move Outward in Empathy and Dignity

If you are in a position to lead others to join you, develop an awareness of the needs of women infected with HIV/AIDS and find out what resources are available to them. Bring along with you in this process a core of other leaders who will explore this issue together with you and who are willing to move out in quiet, invisible but genuine action. No announcements of programs and grand visions—just a building of knowledge and real relationships.

Go to listen. Go to learn. Go to serve. Let their stories be told. Hear the story behind the story. Don't focus on the mechanics or the moral issues being raised but the particularities and vulnerabilities of a person's or family's story. Don't go with answers or fixes. Go with humility, compassion, gentleness. Listen with God's heart for the challenges and suffering they carry.

Do this again and again. Reflect with those you trust about what you are learning, hearing, and feeling. What do you notice about what you might typically miss or fail to fully see?

Are there others you want to invite into a response? Who? Why? To what end? What would they do?

Speak in Empathy and Dignity

If you are a teaching leader or preacher, consider carefully how to speak about what you and others you are with are seeing as well as how you are responding. Be cautious about "packaging" your insights or efforts. Let these things emerge in an understated way first—not as a big, trumpeted announcement, but as what it needs to be: a more personally and quietly integrated reality.

As you prepare to teach or preach from the Bible, ask yourself if you are paying adequate attention to issues of human equality as they arise in the narrative of Scripture, and, in particular, in relation to women, children, and others at the margins. What are the personal issues? What are the systemic issues? What does and does not convey equality and dignity to those who are vulnerable, in word and in action?

What biblical books or portions of Scripture might be the most helpful to consider preaching on as a series concerning the meaning and dignity of being human? How would you develop such a series? Or how might you develop a set of Bible studies or classes for your congregation? What will help them hear the truth most?

These are matters that require wisdom and need to arise as deep conviction in your own life. It is a process of transformation. Be patient. Don't make all this a headline or broadcast. Take the long view, and practice this pursuit of understanding daily, first and foremost, in your own life and relationships.

Act in Empathy and Dignity

Decide to act in concrete ways that are relevant to the needs you seek to respond to, keeping in mind the pace and gifts of people in your congregation. All of these suggestions could be carried out at your church setting or in some other location that might be more appropriate and sensitive toward the women involved.

- Consider starting a support group for women who are dealing with past or present issues and memories of abuse.

- Consider starting an HIV/AIDS support group for women grappling with these conditions.

- Consider making your congregation a place that offers a regular prayer service for women grappling with HIV/AIDS in their lives and in their families' lives.

- Consider special giving and funding needed to provide medicines and other resources, locally or internationally.

If loving God with all we are and loving our neighbor as ourselves is more than just Christian talk, then it needs to show up in tangible ways: in our hearts, in our words, and in our actions. This book will give you the chance to continue to reflect and grow regarding the meaning and shape of the HIV/AIDS crisis. In my view, this disease can become a lens for seeing how God's people are prepared to live differently as a result of Who has made us and Who loves us. What do our lives and actions demonstrate?

Additional Reading

Labberton, Mark. *The Dangerous Act of Loving Your Neighbor: Seeing Others through the Eyes of Jesus.* Downers Grove, IL: InterVarsity, 2010.
———. *The Dangerous Act of Worship: Living God's Call to Justice.* Downers Grove, IL: InterVarsity, 2007.

2

HIV and AIDS

A Brief Overview

ARTHUR J. AMMANN

"Come to me, all you who are weary and burdened, and I will give you rest. Take my yoke upon you and learn from me, for I am gentle and humble in heart, and you will find rest for your souls. For my yoke is easy and my burden is light." (Matthew 11:28–30)

What Are HIV and AIDS?

HIV (HUMAN IMMUNODEFICIENCY VIRUS) is a very small germ called a *virus*. HIV attacks the body's immune system, which is the part of the body that fights off viruses and other infectious agents. Over time, HIV slowly kills the cells of the immune system, making it so weak that the body can no longer defend itself against infections—even cancer. As the immune system weakens, the person will become sick more often and prone to infections that are difficult to heal.

Although some people do experience illness soon after they are infected with HIV, many people feel well for five to ten years after infection. Because so many years can pass before symptoms develop, most people with HIV feel healthy and do not know they are infected with the virus.

Important! Soon after a person is infected with HIV, he or she can pass the virus to others. It is important to remember that even though a person looks and feels healthy, he or she can still be infected with HIV. There is no way to know if a person is infected with HIV simply by looking at him or her. An HIV test is the only way to confirm HIV infection.

AIDS (Acquired Immune Deficiency Syndrome) develops when someone infected with HIV develops opportunistic infections (OIs). These are certain cancers and severe bacterial, viral, and fungal infections that would not ordinarily cause disease in persons with healthy immune systems. Signs of AIDS vary from person to person and can be different between women and men. Commonly, a person who has AIDS will have infections that last a long time, will lose weight, and may even develop cancer. Good nutrition and some medicines can strengthen the immune system, helping it fight off infection; however, there is no cure for AIDS. Over time, without treatment, the disease will progress, and the body will become too weak to survive. With the newer, more active treatment, antiretroviral drugs (ARVs), the growth of the virus is slowed, and individuals with HIV may live healthier, longer lives. Many individuals with HIV now live into their sixth and seventh decades.

Important! All individuals with AIDS are infected with HIV, but not all individuals with HIV have AIDS. This is important to understand because it is sometimes assumed that only individuals with AIDS (who have symptoms of advanced HIV infection) can transmit HIV. It is also important in understanding the statistics that are published when referring to the HIV epidemic. Since not all HIV infected individual have advance to AIDS the number of individuals world-wide who have HIV will always be greater than the number who have AIDS. Throughout this book HIV will be used to designate infection of an individual with the human immunodeficiency virus. Use of the term AIDS will be limited to individuals who have the advanced complications of HIV infection.

How Is HIV Infection Diagnosed?

HIV is diagnosed by means of a simple blood test. Depending on the person's geographic location, either a rapid HIV test or an enzyme-linked immunosorbent assay (ELISA) test is performed. The rapid HIV test can be done on a saliva or urine sample or on a blood drop from a finger stick. Test results are usually available within hours. Some laboratories perform

ELISA tests, whose results may take several days to obtain. An additional test called HIV polymerase chain reaction (HIV PCR) can detect the presence of the virus in the blood even before the antibody is detected. U.S. and European blood banks use this test as an additional screen to eliminate HIV-infected blood, as the viruses are sometimes present even without the antibody test's being positive.

Approximately 30% of the U.S. population has been tested for HIV, either by personal request to a health care provider or due to blood donation or application for disability or health insurance. Even though HIV testing is readily available and inexpensive and can be performed anonymously, approximately 350,000 of the estimated number of individuals infected with HIV in the U.S. have not yet been tested. In the developing world, the number of individuals who are unaware of their infection status reaches into the millions.

How Is HIV Spread?

HIV lives in the bodily fluids of people who are infected. Bodily fluids include blood, semen, vaginal fluid, and breast milk. HIV spreads when the bodily fluid of an infected person enters the body of another person. This means HIV can be spread by:

1. Having unsafe sex (without a condom) with someone who is infected

2. Using unclean needles, syringes, or any tool that pierces or cuts the skin

3. Receiving a blood transfusion with infected blood

4. Getting infected blood into cuts or open wounds

5. Passing the virus from a mother infected with HIV to her baby during birth or by breast-feeding.

How Is HIV Passed from Mother to Child?

Infants have the greatest chance of becoming infected with HIV during labor and delivery. At this time, the baby is exposed to the mother's blood and vaginal secretions. HIV may also be transmitted to infants from breast milk. The risk of HIV transmission increases with:

1. Mixed feeding (giving both breast milk and artificial feeds)

2. Cracked nipples

3. Sores in the baby's mouth

4. Breast-feeding for a prolonged period (i.e., more than one year)

5. Poor maternal health and nutrition

6. A large amount of HIV virus in the mother's body (high viral load). The mother is likely to have a high viral load if she was infected with HIV in the last three months or if she shows signs of AIDS.

Not all infants born to mothers with HIV become infected with the virus. Without treatment, 25% of infants become infected and go on to develop AIDS. Seventy-five percent remain uninfected for the remainder of their lives. If those who are infected do not receive treatment, the mortality rate is 50% by one year of age.

Transmission of HIV during labor and delivery is reduced by more than 98% in developed countries through use of a combination of drugs called *highly active antiretroviral treatment (HAART)* given to the mother during pregnancy and to the baby after delivery, along with formula feeding of the infant. As HAART becomes more available, and as more women with HIV are treated during pregnancy and beyond, transmission rates in developing countries should fall to less than 2%, even when the babies are breastfed.

How Is HIV Not Spread?

Outside of the human body, HIV becomes very weak and can only live for a few minutes. It cannot live on its own in the air or in water. This means you *cannot* give or get HIV by touching, hugging, kissing, or sharing food, clothes, towels, toilets, beds, or blankets. Insects such as mosquitoes do not transmit HIV.

Women and HIV

Women are more easily infected with HIV than men because, during sex, the man's semen can enter the woman's vagina—exposing a large surface area to the virus and remaining in her body for a long time. A young girl is more susceptible to HIV infection than an older woman, as the lining of the vaginal wall is thinner.

If a man's semen is infected with HIV, the virus can pass into the woman's body through her vagina or cervix. If she has cuts or sores in either area, she is even more likely to become infected.

Men who are circumcised are less likely to get HIV. Although the reason for this is not entirely clear, it is hypothesized that removal of the foreskin results in the removal of an area of viral infection and growth. There is no evidence to suggest that female sexual partners of circumcised men with HIV are less likely to become infected.

Cultural, religious, political, legal, and economic circumstances generally place women at high risk for sexual transmission of HIV. Partner notification and legal remedies have potential for protecting women against infection. Currently, more than 50% of HIV infections are in women, most of whom are of childbearing age.

How Is HIV Treated?

Drugs to treat HIV are called *antiretrovirals*. They can control HIV infection and delay the onset of AIDS and death but cannot cure infection. Treatment with three or more HAART drugs can extend life by decades. There are currently more than 30 drugs and combinations of drugs that are administered in various ways for treatment—even once-a-day treatment. Not all drugs are available in resource-poor countries. HIV resistance to drugs has made treatment complex, and a strict adherence to a specific treatment regimen is necessary. There is no vaccine to prevent or treat HIV.

As costs escalate for treating the increasing number of individuals with HIV, prevention is essential. HIV treatment benefits both individuals and the general public health. Treatment of those with HIV greatly reduces the potential for transmission of HIV to those without infection. Mothers with HIV who are undergoing treatment experience longer and healthier lives, allowing them to continue to care for their families and keeping millions of children from becoming orphaned—which currently occurs every year. Treatment of HIV also prevents infections *other* than HIV, thereby reducing the cost of treating the complications of HIV. Many of these additional infections, such as tuberculosis, require hospitalization or extensive treatment.

Advances in prevention and treatment have resulted in dramatic changes in the HIV epidemic. Education and subsequent behavior change have effected decreases in new infections in more than 56 countries to date. New infections fell to 2.7 million in 2010, from a peak of 3.2 million three years previously. Treatment of pregnant women with HIV results in fewer than 2% of their infants becoming infected. Early initiation of HAART for individuals with HIV results in healthy and productive lives. Along with these advancements, however, there is still much to be done, especially for women and children, who require our careful protection and advocacy. For those of us who believe in the teachings of Jesus, we must urge all Christians as well as non-Christians to treat those already infected with compassion.

Additional Reading

HIV InSite: Comprehensive, Up-to-Date Information on HIV/AIDS Treatment, Prevention, and Policy from the University of California San Francisco. Online: http://hivinsite.ucsf.edu.

Volberding, Paul, et al., editors *Sande's HIV/AIDS Medicine: Medical Management of AIDS 2012*. Philadelphia: Saunders Elsevier, 2012.

Whiteside, Alan. *HIV/AIDS: A Very Short Introduction*. Oxford: Oxford University Press, 2008.

Women, Children, and HIV: Resources for Prevention and Treatment (UCSF). Online: http://www.womenchildrenhiv.org.

3

A "Christian" Response to Epidemics?

Theological and Historical Considerations

DARREL W. AMUNDSEN

WHEN ZACCHAEUS WAS SINGLED out by Jesus as the one with whom he wished to dine and lodge, the crowd was indignant. Zacchaeus was a "sinner," a Jew who, as a tax collector for the hated Romans, had sold his nation and his soul for material gain. Jesus's unexpected call stirred him to an immediate and tangible repentance: "Look, Lord! Here and now I give half of my possessions to the poor, and if I have cheated anybody out of anything, I will pay back four times the amount" (Luke 19:8). His giving half of his possessions to the poor flowed from a conscience awakened to a moral imperative central to the Hebrew Scriptures: God's command for his people to manifest his character by doing justice and showing mercy to the poor.

God's love for the "quartet of the vulnerable"—the poor, the widow, the orphan, and the sojourner—is a recurring theme in the Old Testament. He regularly commanded his people to demonstrate that same love. They should neither oppress the poor nor neglect them, but provide for them tangibly. "The poor" is a broad category that includes the widow, the orphan, and the sojourner. The most common Hebrew word for "poor" is *'ani*, which also means "weak" or "afflicted." The *'ani* is primarily a person suffering some kind of distress, including sickness or disability, though the primary feature is being destitute of material resources, which exacerbates one's other afflictions. Such people are vulnerable and dependent. Hence, *'ani* can also mean "lowly" or "humble." They would, by God's design, always be in the land to provide those who were materially better off the opportunity to manifest God's character by providing them with a refuge and caring for them (cf. Deuteronomy 15:11). They also provided a spiritual lesson: Just as the poor (including widows, orphans, and sojourners) are needy, vulnerable, lowly, and dependent, so also should all of God's people be, when it comes to their relationship with him. Furthermore, while the poor in the era covered by the Old Testament tended to remain faithful to God, the rich tended to be attracted to pagan deities. Poverty and godliness, wealth and apostasy tended to go together. Though the care of the poor is not the major focus of the Old Testament, the sins of oppressing or neglecting the poor were symptoms of Israel's apostasy that precipitated God's judgment, culminating in the captivity and deportation of Israel and, later, of Judea. Now, five centuries after the return of a remnant from exile, the Jews of Jesus's time recognized their responsibility to the poor as a fundamental obligation. Hence Zacchaeus's response to Jesus's call.

The dominant message of the New Testament is encapsulated by Jesus's reaction to Zacchaeus's repentance: "For the Son of Man came to seek and to save what was lost" (Luke 19:10). Jesus's preaching focused on repentance and salvation—from sin to righteousness. His injunctions to live a life pleasing to God included caring for the poor and the weak. Not only did Jesus excoriate the religious hypocrites who "devour widows' houses" (Mark 12:40), but he illustrated the scope of mercy that God demanded when, during a discussion of the commandment to love one's neighbor as oneself (Leviticus 19:18), he responded with a parable to a lawyer's question: "Who is my neighbor?"

A Samaritan, who belonged to an ethnic group hated by the Jews, saw a Jew who had been beaten by robbers and left beside the road to die. Two Jews, a priest and a Levite, had already passed by without helping the unconscious Jew. The Samaritan felt compassion, nursed the Jew's wounds, and provided for his continued care. Jesus asked the lawyer, "'Which of these three do you think was a neighbor to the man who fell into the hands of robbers?'" When he answered, "'The one who had mercy on him,'" Jesus said, "'Go and do likewise'" (Luke 10:36–37).

In depicting a despised Samaritan showing greater righteousness than the priest and Levite, who ignored their fellow countryman's dire need, Jesus taught that while one's first responsibility to show mercy is to those within one's community, one is also obliged to seek to help those outside one's normal ambit as occasions arise. As Paul later wrote to the Galatians, "Therefore, as we have opportunity, let us do good to all people, especially to those who belong to the family of believers" (Galatians 6:10). And in "the family of believers" the old distinctions were abolished—ethnic: neither Jew nor Gentile; legal: neither slave nor free; and gender: neither male nor female; "for you are all one in Christ Jesus" (Galatians 3:28).

The parable of the "good Samaritan" provides a model of practical mercy to be extended to men and women whose inherent value to God is so great that his incarnate Son not only made the ultimate sacrifice to redeem them but also, during his ministry, entered into their suffering and alleviated it through healing their diseases. Because of the strong philanthropic motivation inherent in the Gospel, concern for others was shown not only in a desire for the salvation of lost sinners, but also in providing help for those in physical need. What forms should this help take? Jesus gave some examples in his discourse on the last judgment. He told his disciples that he will say to the righteous, "'For I was hungry and you gave me something to eat, I was thirsty and you gave me something to drink, I was a stranger and you invited me in, I needed clothes and you clothed me, I was sick and you looked after me, I was in prison and you came to visit me . . . Whatever you did for one of the least of these brothers of mine, you did for me'" (Matthew 25:35–40).

"I was sick and you looked after me." The Greek verb "to be sick" (*astheneo*) and its cognate noun and adjective have as their basic meaning "weak; weakness." Though the word group is sometimes used metaphorically, the primary meaning is physical infirmity or sickness. For example, the word group appears seven times in the book of Acts. In six of these, "sickness" is clearly the meaning. In Acts 20:35, Paul says to the Ephesian elders, "By this kind of hard work we must help the weak." While the weak here would not be limited to the sick, it would include them, and, given the primary meaning of the word, the sick or infirm would be the first to come to mind.

All these have in common a need that is either a result of poverty or exacerbated by it. Take the sick. Those of very limited means are especially destitute when ill. Looking after the sick here is more than simply comforting them. The Greek verb is *episkeptomai*, which means "visit," typically with a view to caring for those in need by looking after and providing for them. This verb is used to express God's gracious visitation of spiritually destitute humanity by bringing salvation: "'What is man that you are mindful of him, the son of man that you care for [i.e., visit] him?'" (Hebrews 2:6) The same verb is used in James 1:27: "Religion that God our Father accepts as pure and faultless is this: to look after [i.e., care for] orphans and widows in their distress and to keep oneself from being polluted by the world."

The duty to care for the sick became a hallmark of early Christianity, and it caught the attention of pagans for whom such a moral obligation (outside one's immediate family) was quite alien. In the words of Henry Sigerist, a celebrated medical historian, Christianity introduced "the most revolutionary and decisive change in the attitude of society toward the sick. Christianity came into the world as the religion of healing, as the joyful Gospel of the Redeemer and Redemption. It addressed itself to the disinherited, to the sick and the afflicted . . . It became the duty of the Christian to attend to the sick and poor of the community . . . The social position of the sick man thus became fundamentally different from what it had been before. He assumed a preferential position which has been his ever since."

The history of Christianity is rich with examples of spiritually motivated charitable care of the sick, especially of the sick who were poor and hence unable to provide for themselves; the caregivers ranging from individuals to institutions; from small, localized groups to large international organizations. It is, however, easy to overlook just how remarkable this development was. A sentiment (perhaps inherent in fallen human nature) commonly held by people of diverse cultures is that those who prosper and are healthy are favored by God or the gods, and those who are afflicted with deprivations, disabilities, and disease are recipients of divine displeasure. This was certainly the prevailing view of the pagan cultures into which Christianity spread. It was also generally true of the culture in which Christianity arose, since the Hebrew Scriptures fostered such an understanding by the connection between sin and suffering in the account of the Fall: Because of Adam's sin, all material evil—including emotional and physical suffering, sickness, and death—became part of the human experience (Genesis 3:16–19). This connection between sickness and sin was not only reinforced by examples of individuals whose afflictions are specified as punishment for their sins (e.g., Genesis 38:7; Numbers 12:1–16; 2 Samuel 12:15–18; 2 Kings 5:25–27; and 2 Chronicles 21:11–18; and 26:16–21), but it was clearly articulated as God's sovereign prerogative—"See now that I myself am he. There is no god besides me. I put to death and I bring to life, I have wounded and I will heal, and no one can deliver out of my hand" (Deuteronomy 32:39)—most graphically in the Mosaic covenant between

God and his chosen people. Spelled out in Exodus 23 and in much greater detail in Deuteronomy 6–8 are the blessings promised to the people if they love the Lord their God and are faithful and obedient to him, and curses if they flout his love, disobey his commands, and worship and serve other gods. The curses run a horrendous gamut, from horrible diseases to cannibalism to exile and being auctioned as slaves where there are no buyers. The blessings, in stark contrast, include prosperity, fertility, longevity, victory over their enemies, and the absence of illness in the land: "The LORD will take away from you all sickness, and none of the evil diseases of Egypt, which you knew, will he inflict on you, but he will lay them on all who hate you" (Deuteronomy 7:15; cf. Exodus 23:25–26).

It is not surprising that when Jesus and his disciples encountered a man born blind, the disciples asked, "'Rabbi, who sinned, this man or his parents, that he was born blind?'" (John 9:2), so deeply ingrained in Jewish thought was the connection between sickness and sin. Such a prejudice betrayed a failure to see that what appeared to be a fixed cause-and-effect relationship between sin and sickness was not nearly that simple; for often the righteous suffered, not only being persecuted by their own countrymen, but also, it would seem, directly from the hand of God himself. For example, the prophet Elisha died of an unspecified illness (2 Kings 13:14), King Hezekiah and the prophet Daniel were both afflicted with illness (2 Kings 20:1–11; Daniel 8:27), and, of course, there was Job, whose sufferings were exacerbated by the insistence of his friends that his sundry afflictions were punishment for his sins. There are so many instances in the Old Testament in which what seemed so clear was blurred by the reality that the righteous did suffer, often without explanation. This inexplicable suffering caused considerable anguish (see, e.g., Psalms 37 and 88) and forced the sufferer to wait in the darkness with Job and Habakkuk until he could say with the latter, "Though the fig tree does not bud and there are no grapes on the vines, though the olive crop fails, and the fields produce no food, though there are no sheep in the pen and no cattle in the stalls, yet I will rejoice in the Lord, I will be joyful in God my Savior. The Sovereign LORD is my strength; he makes my feet like the feet of a deer, he enables me to go on the heights" (Habakkuk 3:17–19).

The experience of Asaph in Psalm 73 is richly instructive. When he viewed the health and prosperity of the wicked and contemplated his own afflictions, likely including sickness, he thought, "This is what the wicked are like—always carefree, they increase in wealth. Surely in vain have I kept my heart pure; in vain have I washed my hands in innocence. All day long I have been plagued; I have been punished every morning. If I had said, 'I will speak thus,' I would have betrayed your children. When I tried to understand all this, it was oppressive to me till I entered the sanctuary of God; then I understood their final destiny" (Psalm 73:12–17). But Asaph held himself back from such profanity, went into the sanctuary of God, and there caught a glimpse of the Eternal that enabled him finally to say, "Whom have I in heaven but you? And earth has nothing I desire besides you. My flesh and my heart may fail, but God is the strength of my heart and my portion forever" (Psalm 73:25–26).

Thus, in preparation for the revelation of the Suffering Servant, their as-yet-unknown and unrevealed Redeemer, was God slowly weaning his people from the material and temporal to the spiritual and eternal. He was despised and rejected of men, a man of sorrows and acquainted with grief, the antithesis of the Messiah whom the Jewish people were anticipating. It was only after the cross and resurrection that Jesus's disciples could see their Redeemer in his redemptive suffering and could grasp that, although being God's own son, even he "learned obedience from what he suffered" (Hebrews 5:8). Suffering took on a potentially salubrious quality only dimly adumbrated in the Old Testament. And such suffering included sickness; and the sinful stigma of sickness, if not entirely removed, was at least substantially lessened.

Although in the New Testament there are occasional instances in which sickness, physical impairment, or sudden death is specified as punishment for sin (e.g. Luke 1:5–23; Acts 5:1–11; 12:20–23; 13:4–12; 1 Corinthians 5:5; and 11:27–32), in the ministry of Jesus the direct causal link between individual sickness and personal sin is called into question. On one occasion Jesus forgave a paralytic's sins before healing him, although no connection between the forgiveness and healing appears even to be implied (Matthew 9:1–8 and parallels). He commanded another paralytic, in this case *after* healing him, "Stop sinning or something worse may happen to you" (John 5:14). Although numerous healings are recorded in the Gospels, in no other instances is sin mentioned. This speaks loudly of Jesus's attitude about the common assumption that individual sickness is punishment for personal sin. He said of Lazarus's sickness: "'This sickness will not end in death. No, it is for God's glory so that God's Son may be glorified through it" (John 11:4). Note Jesus's response to his disciples' question about a man born blind: "His disciples asked him, 'Rabbi, who sinned, this man or his parents, that he was born blind?' 'Neither this man nor his parents sinned,' said Jesus, 'but this happened so that the work of God might be displayed in his life'" (John 9:2–3). While Jesus's response does not preclude some causal relationship between personal sin and individual sicknesses, it shows that he regarded blanket, judgmental assessments as tenuous at best.

Throughout the Old Testament, the one form of sickness that was patently explicated as God's judgment for sin is what was imprecisely called "pestilence" or "plague," as several Hebrew nouns, most notably *deber*, are rendered. Sometimes these words, when translated as "plague," are used metaphorically or refer to afflictions other than sickness, sent by God for a specific purpose. Most notably in this category are the ten "plagues" on the Egyptians recorded in Exodus 7–12 and the "plague" of serpents in Numbers 21:4–9 sent as a punishment for the murmuring discontentment of the people. Usually, however, whether translated as "plague" or "pestilence," the affliction was a devastating disease that smote either a specific group (e.g., the ten cowardly spies in Numbers 14) or, more commonly, the population at large. The latter is of two categories—that recorded as historical event and that threatened or prophesied. When David sinned by conducting a census contrary to God's will, he was given a choice, "Go and tell David, 'This is what the LORD says: I am giving you three options. Choose one of them for me to carry out against you.'" So Gad went to David and said to him, "Shall there come upon you three years of famine in your land? Or three months of fleeing from your enemies while they pursue you? Or three days of plague in your land? Now then, think it over and decide how I should answer the one who sent me" (2 Samuel 24:12–13). He chose pestilence, and 70,000 Israelites died before the Lord stayed his hand in response to David's plea for mercy on the innocent being afflicted for his sin (2 Samuel 24 and 1 Chronicles 21).

This triad of disasters—the sword, famine, and pestilence—appears frequently in the Old Testament, especially in the prophecies of Jeremiah and Ezekiel. Such prophecies are rooted in the curses of the Mosaic covenant, discussed above, as some of the most dramatically devastating judgments that God would visit upon his people if they spurned his love; defied the commandments that he had given for their spiritual, material, and physical well-being; and diverted their worship into the vile practices of their pagan neighbors. The curses of the Mosaic covenant seem less like warnings than like prophecy, for Israel had shown herself to be rebellious and stubborn immediately after the Exodus, even before the giving of the

Mosaic covenant. As God said through Isaiah, "You have neither heard nor understood; from of old your ear has not been open. Well do I know how treacherous you are; you were called a rebel from birth" (Isaiah 48:8). But in spite of her obstinacy and disobedience, her idolatry and spurning of him, he, in his longsuffering and patience, allowed her to retain possession of the land generation after generation before imposing on her the promised afflictions culminating in her being led away into captivity.

When plague or pestilence occurs or is threatened in the Old Testament, the reader is never left in the dark about God's purposes in inflicting it. Nevertheless, at the time that Old Testament history was unfolding, problems of understanding arose. God's judgment on apostasy was often withheld. The exceedingly wicked within Israel—particularly the rulers—often prospered individually. The righteous were often afflicted by the wicked within the land, and God's judgment was still withheld. When it did come, both the wicked and the righteous were swept away. Considerable consternation arose over this enigma in some of the Psalms. For example, in Psalm 44 this theme is mingled with pleas that God would restore his blessing to those who still were faithful and had not broken the covenant.

The corporate nature of the Mosaic covenant gives both its blessings and curses a quality distinct from any other covenant that does not have as an ultimate end a relationship grounded in faithfulness between God and his people. Further, the suffering that is a consequence of violating the covenant is so concrete as to leave no room for mystery or subtlety. Suffering that results from the curses attached to the Mosaic covenant must be—in essence, if not in manifestation—categorically different from all other suffering within the realm of human experience. Hence, it is reasonable to ask whether it is theologically correct to apply a text such as 2 Chronicles 15:2 ("The LORD is with you when you are with him. If you seek him, he will be found by you, but if you forsake him, he will forsake you") to England, as the Puritan John Owen did. Granted, in the covenant of grace, God's dealings with his people were essentially the same in the seventeenth century A.D. as in the seventeenth century B.C. But God's covenantal relationship with the corporate body of his people under the Mosaic covenant differed from his relationship with seventeenth-century England.

In other words, can one apply the following statement to both nations, as Owen does? "The presence of God with a people, in special providential dispensations for their good, depends on their obediential presence with him in national administrations to his glory: 'The Lord is with you, while ye be with him.'" But surely not to England or to any other nation in the same way as ancient Israel under the Mosaic covenant. At most, the latter can be paradigmatic for the former. But even as a paradigm, it must be treated most circumspectly. One commentator on Deuteronomy remarks that the curse of God "appears to be the inevitable outcome of life that is lived regardless of God, by rejecting a relationship with God whose essence is love." When such reasoning is applied to nations, we have not only bad theology, but bad historiography. When it is applied to individuals, it may well be both theologically inaccurate and cruel. *The blessings and curses of the Mosaic covenant were not simply God's formal articulation of cause-and-effect in divinely ordained natural laws.*

In considering plagues and pestilences, our focus has been on the Old Testament. What does the New Testament have to say about such disasters? The only references to plagues or pestilences in the New Testament are in connection with a variety of other natural disasters and wars that will overtake the wicked when God brings down the curtain on human history. This gives us little help in seeking scriptural guidance for determining God's specific purposes in natural disasters not recorded in Scripture. Yet typically Christians feel a pull to attempt to see God's hand in history. Likely most Christians would agree that history not only has a beginning—God is the Creator not only of the universe, but of time as well—but that history also has an end—God will bring time to an end and history to its conclusion. God is sovereign. He is the grand and ultimate Pilot at the helm of history and is guiding history forward. In due time—in his time—it will reach his goal. God has worked, is working, and will continue to work in human history through general providence and particular providence—that is, direct intervention.

Our knowledge of God's general and particular providence comes through general revelation and special revelation. The history contained in Scripture belongs to the second of these categories, special revelation. All other history is by definition either part of, or essentially and qualitatively similar to, general revelation. Hence, biblical history is essentially and qualitatively different from all other history, and the latter cannot permit anything approaching the same degree of certainty as the former when one seeks to identify and appreciate God's purposes in history. This holds true for recent and current events, which will soon be the stuff of history. Special revelation frequently admonishes us against presumption in assessing God's ways: "'For my thoughts are not your thoughts, neither are your ways my ways,' declares the LORD. 'As the heavens are higher than the earth, so are my ways higher than your ways and my thoughts than your thoughts'" (Isaiah 55:8–9). "Oh, the depth of the riches of the wisdom and knowledge of God! How unsearchable his judgments, and his paths beyond tracing out!" (Romans 11:33).

Jesus cautioned against—"cautioned" is too mild a word—*condemned* judgmental assessments of God's purposes: "Now there were some present at that time who told Jesus about the Galileans whose blood Pilate had mixed with their sacrifices. Jesus answered, 'Do you think that these Galileans were worse sinners than all the other Galileans because they suffered this way? I tell you, no! But unless you repent, you too will all perish. Or those eighteen who died when the tower in Siloam fell on them—do you think they were more guilty than all the others living in Jerusalem? I tell you, no! But unless you repent, you too will all perish'" (Luke 13:1–5).

In a sermon preached in September 1861, after a horrible accident about which the evangelical press in Britain made sweeping judgmental pronouncements, C. H. Spurgeon said,

> The visible providence of God has no respect of persons . . . Although your faith assures you that the ultimate result of providence will work out only good to the people of God, yet your life, though it be but a brief part of the Divine drama of history, must have taught you that providence does not outwardly discriminate between the righteous and the wicked—that the righteous perish suddenly as well as the wicked—that the plague knows no difference between the sinner and the saint—and that the sword of war is alike pitiless to the sons of God and the sons of Belial . . . The idea that whenever an accident occurs we are to look upon it as a judgment from God *would make the providence of God to be, instead of a great deep, a very shallow pool.* Why, any child can [then] understand the providence of God . . . But Scripture teaches us that providence is a great depth in which the human intellect may swim and dive, but it can neither find a bottom nor a shore, and if you and I pretend that we can find out the reasons of providence, and twist the dispensations of God over our fingers, we only prove our folly, but we do not prove that we have begun to understand the ways of God . . . Only [God] knoweth the end from the beginning, only he understands what are the great results, and what is the great reason for which the world was made, and for which he permits both good and evil to occur. Think not that you know the ways of God; it is to degrade providence, and to bring God down

to the level of men, when you pretend that you can understand these calamities and find out the secret designs of wisdom.

We who are Christians should always heed Spurgeon's sagacious counsel, for we, as Christians, have presuppositions and understanding that can stimulate within us a frightening capacity for judgmentalism and censoriousness far greater than the typical secularist. We have the desire—perhaps even the obligation—to be aware of God in history and in recent and current events. This practice can lead us to identify God's purposes sometimes with a degree of certainty that should alarm us. It is here that Christians can do a great deal of harm to themselves, to each other, and to God's general cause. Some possess an over-assurance—in the words of two Christian historians, George Marsden and Frank Roberts, "a disposition to play down the complexity and ambiguity of history and to emphasize the clarity of the divine plan and purpose of events of the past." And this applies, as I have emphasized above, also to current events. This effrontery often has been and is mingled with a kind of patriotism that, when bathed in poor theology, produces a particularly odious jingoism.

The history of epidemiology is rife with examples of Christians responding to epidemics with an appalling degree of judgmental certitude, castigating particular groups as the objects of God's wrath that caused a ravaging of the entire community. Sometimes it was communities of foreigners or minority ethnic groups—e.g., Jews—living in their midst. Tolerating heretics in the community was frequently thought to be the reason why God sent epidemics. On some occasions, Catholics saw God's judgment visited on communities because of Protestants in their midst, and vice versa. In Tudor and Stuart Britain, Anglican and nonconformist pastors at times alternated in making each other responsible for various epidemics, particularly outbreaks of smallpox. Often moral turpitude such as drunkenness or sexual immorality was thought to have precipitated God's wrath, and occasionally particular sins practiced by the wealthy (e.g., extravagantly wasteful self-indulgence in food or fashions). These examples—some of which are amusing, others of which are disturbing—could be multiplied many times over, to no particular profit. All have in common that they arose in communities that were predominantly Christian.

When we look at the development of public health policies and practices in Christian countries or communities, it is difficult to determine whether a policy or practice is distinctly the result of Christian presuppositions or of secular views. For example, sometimes the poor, whose unsanitary living conditions fit nicely with miasmic explanations of the origin and spreading of certain epidemic diseases, were singled out. Likewise, was it a kind of Christian misogyny that, as some historians insist, caused the stigmatization of women as contaminators during the early decades of the syphilis epidemic, or was it the consequence of a fallacious pathological paradigm rigidly applied by an often arrogant medical hierarchy? Women were regarded as the contaminators because men were thought to contract the disease much more easily than women. The woman's matrix [womb, vagina], "being cold, dry, and dense," was regarded as significantly less susceptible to contracting the disease. The membrum virile [penis], "being warm and moist," and having open pores, was viewed as being exceedingly vulnerable to infection. So, it was thought, whereas a man could easily contract the disease by having sexual intercourse with an infected woman—or even with a healthy woman with whom an infected man had recently engaged in coitus—a woman, by contrast, could generally contract the disease sexually only by frequent intercourse with the infected. The conclusion that followed was that women who were infected sexually were promiscuous, and that the majority were prostitutes (a conclusion that shares remarkable similarities to the claim that is currently placed on women with HIV, who although more susceptible to HIV infection than men, and who most often acquire HIV from men, are blamed and ostracized even from the Christian church). This was not the result of Christian misogyny; rather it was the inevitable conclusion of humoral pathology, a paradigm that was created by Greek natural philosophers 2,000 years earlier and that dominated Western medicine until the advent of concepts of specific etiology. The list of seeming discrimination could easily be extended against various groups of people. That was not discrimination at all, but rather the inevitable consequence of morally neutral medical models prevalent in Christian Europe and America.

Historians who castigate Christianity for such actions simply show both their prejudices and their ignorance of some important aspects of medical history. But there are many instances of judgmentalism by Christians available as legitimate objects of criticism, some of which I described above. And we as Christians should take care not to add to that list by our own conduct. Christian moral judgments and assessments usually tend to be condemnatory, typically of others rather than ourselves. We must guard against that. And we ought to be infinitely more understanding than secularists of why people act as they do, why they struggle within the tangle of perplexities and paradoxes of life as they do. Whether looking at the past or the present, we ought to have an increased sensitivity to the mysteries of God's ways, an increased sense of our own finitude and of the limitations of our understanding, even though we have the inestimable advantage of spiritual life and spiritual insight.

Finally, we owe an overwhelming thankfulness for the relationship of love, trust, faith, and hope into which the almighty Creator of all things has drawn us. Then even a glimpse into our own hearts should be sufficient to engender in us a reluctance to judge and a stimulus to love, sympathize, and understand, in the deepest sense of these words. Many of our Christian brothers and sisters have shown this love in their selfless care of the destitute during epidemics. During the unidentifiable plagues that occurred in the early centuries, many Christians put themselves at considerable risk in caring for pagans who were deserted by kith and kin—those very pagans who had been persecuting Christians as god-haters, whose presence in the Roman Empire had, they thought, caused the gods to send the plagues. Their selflessness and motivation are similar to that of Christians today who provide a refuge for destitute and forsaken individuals with HIV and who care for others irrespective of gender, race, or manner of contracting disease, motivated, as were their Christians forebears of every generation, to heed the call of their Master "'I was sick and you visited me . . . As you did it to one of the least of these my brothers, you did it to me.'" (Matthew 25:40).

Additional Reading

Amundsen, Darrel W. *Medicine, Society, and Faith in the Ancient and Medieval Worlds.* Baltimore: Johns Hopkins University Press, 1996.

Ferngren, Gary, editor. *The History of Science and Religion in the Western Tradition: An Encyclopedia.* Garland Reference Library of the Humanities. New York. Garland, 2000.

———. *Medicine and Health Care in Early Christianity.* Baltimore: Johns Hopkins University Press, 2009.

Mormando, Franco, and Thomas Worcester, editors. *Piety and Plague: From Byzantium to the Baroque* Kirksville, MO: Truman State University Press, 2007.

Ranger, Terence, and Paul Slack, editors. *Epidemics and Ideas: Essays on the Historical Perception of Pestilence.* Past and Present Pulications. Cambridge: Cambridge University Press, 1992.

4

"Our Women Amazed Us"

The Role of Women in the Story of Redemption

DANIEL B. CLENDENIN

Are Women Human?

THAT'S THE QUESTION THE British writer Dorothy Sayers (1893–1957) posed in two short essays written in 1938. She had more than an academic interest in the question. When she finished Somerville College, Oxford, with first-class honors in modern languages in 1915, they didn't yet grant degrees to women.

The question sounds crazy until you consider the many inhuman things that men have said about women—that they are more susceptible to sin, that they are intellectually inferior to men, and that they are inferior to men not only in body and mind but in soul. Consider these few examples from both secular and church history:

In *Timaeus*, Plato wrote that the fate of men who are "cowards or who lead unrighteous lives" is to be reincarnated as women. In *The Generation of Animals*, Aristotle argued that nature ideally prefers to generate a male, and that the female is a "deformed male . . . Females are imperfect males, accidentally produced by the father's inadequacy." More than a thousand years later, the great Thomas Aquinas would quote this text from Aristotle. And the Jewish historian Josephus (c. 37–100 CE), appealing to the Old Testament, wrote in *Against Apion* that "the woman, says the Law, is in all things inferior to the man."

Down through the ages, many Christians have repeated and justified these sorts of inhuman mischaracterizations of women. Tertullian called women "the devil's gateway," responsible not only for the fall of Adam but also for the death of the Son of God. In his commentary on Genesis, Luther wrote that women are "weaker in body and intellect than men . . . inferior to the man in both honor and dignity." *The Catholic Encyclopedia* of 1913 declared that "the female sex is in some respects inferior to the male sex, both as regards body and soul."

And so, Sayers asks: Are women human?

"Man is willing to accept woman," Sayers wrote, quoting D. H. Lawrence, "as an equal, as a man in skirts, as an angel, a devil, a baby-face, an instrument, a bosom, a womb, a pair of legs, a servant, an encyclopedia, an ideal or an obscenity; the one thing he won't accept her as is a human being, a real human being of the feminine sex." That was the gist of Sayers' radically simple petition: that women be acknowledged as human beings made in the image of God, and only subsequently labeled as a class of human beings qualified by biology, culture, ethnicity, age, economics, nationality, and so on.

Sayers also made an observation about the stories in the gospels that radically subverted the dehumanization of women. Women, she noted, were "the first at the Cradle and the last at the Cross." At every juncture of Jesus's life, from his birth to his death, resurrection, and even ascension, women have played a conspicuous role in the story of redemption.

First at the Cradle, Last at the Cross

We see this reality in Jesus's genealogy, even before he was born. Four infamous women were listed in his genealogy of forty-six names (Matthew 1:1–17). Tamar was widowed twice and then became pregnant by her father-in-law Judah, who mistook her for a temple prostitute. The offspring of this incest were the twin boys Perez and Zerah. Perez is a relative of Jesus (see Ruth 4:18–21). Rahab was a foreigner and a whore who, by her lies, protected the Hebrew spies. She was mentioned only three times in the New Testament: as a hero of faith (Hebrews 11:31), as an exemplar of good works (James 2:25), and as the great-great-grandmother of King David (Matthew 1:5). Ruth was a foreigner and widow who married the wealthy Boaz, King David's great-grandfather. Bathsheba, the subject of David's adulterous passion and murderous cover-up, was the mother of King Solomon. These women were part of Jesus's family of origin.

It's impossible to consider the birth of Jesus without mentioning Mary. When I was in Oxford a few years ago, every evening I left my study carrel and walked down Woodstock Road to the city center and attended the Evensong services at Magdalen College. I loved so many things about those 30 minutes of worship—the quiet, the architecture, the history (Magdalen College was founded in 1448), the smell of the candles that lit the early darkness of October, the boys' choir in robes, and the formal liturgy. But one part of Evensong surprised me: Every single night we sang Mary's "Magnificat" from Luke's gospel. Why did the daily liturgy assign her such prominence? Why is Mary so important?

Protestants question dogmas about Mary that were codified quite recently and that do not enjoy unequivocal biblical support—like her perpetual virginity, her freedom from actual and original sin (Immaculate Conception, 1854), and the idea that she did not die but was taken directly to heaven (Bodily Assumption, 1950). We also get agitated about exalted language that sounds like she is a co-redeemer of humanity. In popular devotion the cult of Mary can drift into excess and superstition. So Protestants emphasize a caveat that both Catholics and Orthodox acknowledge: Christians honor or venerate (*duleia*) Mary as the Mother of God, but we do not worship her (*latreia*), as worship is due to God alone.

Nevertheless, you might argue that no woman has influenced Western history and culture more than Mary. Her "Magnificat," which takes its name from the first word of the text in Latin, is recorded in Luke 1:46–55:

Mary's Song

And Mary said: "My soul glorifies the Lord
and my spirit rejoices in God my Savior,
for he has been mindful of the humble state of his servant.
From now on all generations will call me blessed,
for the Mighty One has done great things for me—holy is his
name.
His mercy extends to those who fear him, from generation to
generation.
He has performed mighty deeds with his arm;
he has scattered those who are proud in their inmost thoughts.
He has brought down rulers from their thrones but has lifted up
the humble.

He has filled the hungry with good things but has sent the rich
away empty.
He has helped his servant Israel, remembering to be merciful
to Abraham and his descendants forever, even as he said to our
fathers." (Luke 1:46–55).

Just how and why do we venerate Mary? Why is she so important for
a truly biblical faith?

Mary was a woman of exemplary faith. She was a peasant girl from
a working-class neighborhood of carpenters in Nazareth, a village so
insignificant that it is not mentioned in the Old Testament, by the historian Josephus, or in the Jewish Talmud. "Can anything good come from
Nazareth?" asked Nathaniel (John 1:46). Her angelic encounter took place
in an unknown, ordinary house, not the temple. When the angel Gabriel
foretold the birth of her son Jesus, Mary responded in words of faith that
have echoed through the centuries: "I am the Lord's servant. May it be to
me as you have said" (Luke 1:38). Her bold belief startled her pregnant
cousin Elizabeth, who exclaimed "in a loud voice": "Blessed are you among
women, and blessed is the child you will bear! . . . Blessed is she who has
believed that what the Lord has said to her will be accomplished!" (Luke
1:42, 45).

Catholics remind us of another "Marian" truth that is easy to overlook but nevertheless stupendous. In some mysterious way, the incarnation
resulted not only from the work of God the Father but also from the will
of the Mother Mary. Numerous church fathers have acknowledged Mary's
active cooperation in the history of salvation. According to Thomas Aquinas (*Summa*, III.30), human redemption depended upon the consent of
the pregnant teenager Mary. She did not ask to bear the Son of God, nor
was she compelled to do so. She might have said no, or, like Zechariah,
responded to Gabriel's staggering annunciation in disbelief. But she did not
shrink from God's call on her life, and instead enriched all humanity by her
willing participation and obedient submission.

Mary was also a woman of prophetic pronouncement. Her "Magnificat" moved from the deeply personal to the explicitly political. God, Mary
proclaimed, "has been mindful of the humble state of his servant . . . for
the Mighty One has done great things for me" (Luke 1:48–49). (This peasant girl, who, a few months later, would bear God's Son, then praised God
because "he has brought down rulers from their thrones but has lifted up
the humble. He has filled the hungry with good things but has sent the rich

away empty" (Luke 1:52–53). I wonder what Herod or Tiberius thought when they heard her words.) The incarnation of the Son of God, Mary announced, meant the inversion of conventional wisdom. Dethroning political power, plundering rich people, and redistributing food supplies signaled a new age and order.

Finally, Eastern Orthodox believers emphasize that the son of Mary would be the Son of God, God made flesh, and so they honor her with the technical term *theotokos* ("bearer of God"). This term, bestowed upon Mary by church fathers since the third century, acknowledges her special role in redemption; she is nothing less than the "Mother of God." But when the term gained official status at the third ecumenical council of Ephesus in 431, the intent was to emphasize the full divinity of the Son more than the privileged status of his mother. Mary did not give birth to a mere man (*christotokos*), as the Nestorians taught; she bore a child who was fully divine.

If you wonder why Catholics and the Orthodox refer to Mary as the "Blessed Virgin," consider the birth narrative of Jesus: "Blessed are you among women," Elizabeth said (Luke 1:42). "From now on all generations shall call me blessed," Mary acknowledged (Luke 1:48). Veneration of the Mother of God leads to exaltation of the Son of God, which is precisely the message of Christmas: "My soul glorifies the Lord and my spirit rejoices in God my Savior" (Luke 1:46–47).

After these birth narratives, we also see the central role of women in the life and ministry of Jesus. Luke's gospel punctuated that point: "Jesus traveled about from one town and village to another, proclaiming the good news of the kingdom of God. The Twelve were with him, and also some women who had been cured of evil spirits and diseases: Mary (called Magdalene) from whom seven demons had come out; Joanna the wife of Cuza, the manager of Herod's household; Susanna; and many other women. These women were helping to support them out of their own means" (Luke 8:1–3).

The prominence of women in the life of Jesus has not only been deeply embedded in the gospels but was also highly unusual for that time and place. In one incident, the disciples expressed amazement that Jesus even spoke to a woman (John 4:27; see below). Respected rabbis would not have associated with women as Jesus did, and women were not allowed to study the Torah. A well-known prayer found in three rabbinic traditions (Tosephta, Palestinian/Jerusalem Talmud, and the Babylonian Talmud) thus thanked God for not being born a Gentile, a woman, or an ignorant man—none of whom enjoyed the privilege of studying the Torah.

Today these women mentioned by Luke are barely known to us: Mary Magdalene was mentioned several times in the gospels. Joanna was a witness to the resurrection (Luke 24:10), while the identities of her husband Cuza, Susanna, and the "many other women" who supported Jesus remain lost to history. In Luke's day they must have been well-known people of financial means who had left their husbands and families in order to underwrite a sizeable group of itinerating evangelists. Perhaps they were some of those first believers who sold their lands and houses and used the money to support the Jesus movement (Acts 4:34). Whatever the particulars, they were, as the poker expression puts it, "all in."

The story of the woman at the well is deeply instructive about the role of women in the story of redemption. Like the woman caught in the act of adultery (John 8), the story of Jesus's encounter with the Samaritan woman at the well reminds us that the kingdom he inaugurated is a realm of inclusion, not exclusion; dignity, not denigration; empowerment rather than exploitation; and affirmation rather than marginalization. His simple request for a drink of water provoked a dialogue with a marginalized woman that teaches us that Jesus does not desire any human being to shrivel and die from a parched soul. Rather, he longs to quench the deepest needs and desires of each one of us with the "living water" of his Spirit.

As Jesus traveled from Judea to Galilee, he stopped in the town of Sychar around noontime, tired and thirsty from the journey. He sat down by a well and asked a Samaritan woman for a drink of water. That Jesus, a Jew, would talk to a Samaritan shocked the woman (John 4:9). That he would talk to a woman surprised his own disciples (4:27). In fact, through death or divorce, this woman had burned through five marriages and was then living with a boyfriend, not a husband (4:18).

When you connect the dots of her story, you realize that, in her one person, this woman epitomized the many ways that society marginalizes people. Jesus shatters all the taboos that held sway then (and now)—gender discrimination, ritual purity (sharing a drinking cup with a Samaritan), socioeconomic poverty (any woman married five times was likely poor), religious hostility, and the moral stigma of serial marriages.

In marked contrast to the male rabbi–scholar Nicodemus in the previous chapter (John 3), the Samaritan woman displayed spiritual thirst, candor about her past, and genuine insight. She longed not only for real water, but for the "living water" (John 4:11) that Jesus offered her—so much so that in her excitement she forgot her water jar when she returned to town (4:28). This thoroughly powerless woman made such a powerful impression upon Jesus and her own neighbors that John included an interesting eyewitness detail about Jesus's itinerary: Upon the neighbors' request, "he stayed two days" in Sychar (4:40). The woman embraced Jesus as the Messiah, her witness converted many fellow Samaritans in town (4:39), and she became the cause of the story's punch line: "We no longer believe just because of what you said; now we have heard for ourselves, and we really know that this man is the Savior of the world" (4:42).

As in so many gospel stories about God's alternative community, John 4 subverts and reverses conventional human wisdom and power relations. Jesus not only engaged a disreputable, ostracized, foreign woman; he cast her as the hero of the story, as a symbol of life in his kingdom, and as an ardent witness to his universal lordship. In so doing, he warns us of religiosity that turns a deaf ear to the disenfranchised, and that masks an otherwise smug, exclusionary, and self-serving faith.

The Integral Role of Widows Throughout History

As one other example of the importance of women in the ministry of Jesus, consider the prominence of widows in the gospels, who likewise epitomize the reversals and subversions of power in God's kingdom. Widows in particular occupy a major role in this story; the Greek word for "widow" (*chera*) occurs about twenty-five times in the New Testament.

That God cares for widows—and that his people should, too—is a prominent theme throughout the Bible. One story of a nameless widow reverses our conventions: At the temple, Jesus observed "many rich people" making large donations (Mark 12:41). In stark contrast, a poor widow's gift amounted to "only a fraction of a penny" (12:42). Whereas the rich gave out of the convenience of their surplus, said Jesus, "this poor widow has put more into the treasury than all the others. They all gave out of their wealth; but she, out of her poverty, put in everything—all she had to live on" (12:43–44).

In this story, the woman was not a victim but an exemplar. She embodied the extravagant benefactor instead of the vulnerable beneficiary. This nameless widow in the Gospel reminds us of other famous widows in the Old Testament. For instance, the book of Ruth is in fact a story of three widows: the Israelite Naomi, who fled Israel to Moab to escape famine, and her two foreign daughters-in-law, Orpah and Ruth. After ten years in Moab, and despite Naomi's protests, Ruth returned with her to Israel. In Bethlehem, Ruth was the foreigner from an enemy country. She was childless. She was widowed from a mixed marriage. But she vowed to cling to Naomi, to her Hebrew people, and to their God. Ruth secured an economic livelihood for her mother-in-law and herself by gleaning in the fields among the hired hands. She followed Naomi's plan to ingratiate herself to Boaz, the owner of the fields where she gleaned. All of Bethlehem knew this foreign widow as a "woman of noble character" (Ruth 3:11).

Boaz was both a wealthy man and a near relative to Naomi's deceased husband Elimelech. As such, he not only had the means but also the obligation to "redeem" Ruth (and, in the process, Naomi). Another relative was even closer to Naomi than Boaz, but when he refused to redeem Ruth, he cleared the way for Boaz. This second mixed marriage conceived a son, Obed, the grandfather of King David. Ruth's improbable story culminates when we meet her again on the very first page of the New Testament as a forebear of Christ himself (Matthew 1:5).

As with Ruth, we encounter the widow of Zarephath (1 Kings 17) at a pivotal juncture in Israel's history, and then we meet her again in the New Testament (Luke 4). Her story shows how God can turn bold and simple obedience into merciful and extravagant miracles.

God told the prophet Elijah to travel far out of his way to Zarephath, in the land of Sidon, where he would meet a foreign widow who would show him hospitality. The entire area had been suffering an excruciating famine for three and a half years, due to the unspeakable wickedness of the day. After Elijah's arrival, this widow was willing, through extreme faith, to serve Elijah her very last morsel of food—a handful of meal and a bit of oil—even though she believed directly that she and her son would starve to death. Her obedience to God and her generosity toward Elijah effected a continual stream of miracles: Day after day, her jar of meal and her jug of oil never became empty.

After hosting Elijah in her home for some time, this widow discovered that her son, who was ill, had died. This woman, who had endured years of famine, who had trusted God with her last meal in giving it away, and who had witnessed the resultant miracles, was flooded with desperation. Where was God when she needed him (1 Kings 17:18)? Elijah, through pleading with God over and over, finally presented this woman with the body of her living, breathing boy. God's faithfulness reigned in this woman's life, and *her* faithfulness allowed God to manifest immeasurable mercy.

> Some time later the son of the woman who owned the house became ill. He grew worse and worse, and finally stopped breathing.
>
> She said to Elijah, "What do you have against me, man of God? Did you come to remind me of my sin and kill my son?"
>
> "Give me your son," Elijah replied. He took him from her arms, carried him to the upper room where he was staying, and laid him on his bed.
>
> Then he cried out to the LORD, "O LORD my God, have you brought tragedy also upon this widow I am staying with, by causing her son to die?"
>
> Then he stretched himself out on the boy three times and cried to the LORD, "O LORD my God, let this boy's life return to him!"
>
> The LORD heard Elijah's cry, and the boy's life returned to him, and he lived.
>
> Elijah picked up the child and carried him down from the room into the house. He gave him to his mother and said, "Look, your son is alive!"
>
> Then the woman said to Elijah, "Now I know that you are a man of God and that the word of the LORD from your mouth is the truth." (1 Kings 17:17–24).

This narrative of a nameless, alien widow and a Hebrew prophet offering each other mutual care across nationalistic boundaries assumed such central importance in Israel's sacred storytelling that Jesus repeated it a thousand years later. The impact was the same: The listeners were outraged at the role reversals. "'I assure you that there were many widows in Israel in Elijah's time,'" said Jesus, "'when the sky was shut for three and a half years and there was a severe famine throughout the land. Yet Elijah was not sent to any of them, but to a widow in Zarephath in the region of [enemy] Sidon . . .' All the people in the synagogue were furious when they heard this" (Luke 4:25–28). Clearly, Jesus has no problem commending those who exhibit faith—no matter their race, class, or marital status.

There are remarkable similarities between the story of Elijah and the widow in Zarephath and the story of Jesus and the Samaritan woman at the well. Both women were non-Jews, both were concerned about their past, and both were offered miraculous sustenance. The amount of scriptural space given to these two narratives, considering that they are about two women whose names are not even mentioned, suggests that God and Jesus want us to engage women in need, especially widows. In both of these particular instances, we are given the impression that the prophet Elijah and Jesus "had to" visit the women, and, as mentioned previously, they went out of their way to do so.

"The Maker of heaven and earth," as God is called in Psalm 146, additionally demonstrates his desires and his power in ways subtler than resurrecting the dead. He's biased on behalf of the oppressed. He feeds the hungry, frees prisoners, and heals the blind. He lifts up those who are weighted down. He defends foreigners, protects the orphan, and sustains the widow. Many of these widows, as we've been discussing, have themselves played conspicuous roles in the proliferation of God's kingdom here on earth.

These stories about widows are especially compelling because many of the earliest Christians came from the lower socioeconomic classes of Rome. The harsh critic Celsus, for example, combined socioeconomic snobbery with intellectual elitism:

> In some private homes we find people who work with wool and rags, and cobblers, that is, the least cultured and most ignorant kind. Before the head of the household they dare not utter a word. But as soon as they can take the children aside or some women who are as ignorant as they are, they speak wonders . . . If you really wish to know the truth, leave your teachers and your father, and go with the women and the children to the women's quarters, or to the cobbler's shop, or to the tannery, and there you will learn the perfect life. It is thus that these Christians find those who will believe them.

We typically don't turn to widows for wisdom. But what Celsus considered a criticism was for Paul an insight about living in the kingdom of God: "God chose the foolish things of the world to shame the wise; God chose the weak things of the world to shame the strong. He chose the lowly things of this world and the despised things—and the things that are not—to nullify the things that are, so that no one may boast before him" (1 Corinthians 1:27–29).

The Enduring Faithfulness of Jesus's Female Friends

Women were as prominent at the death, resurrection, and ascension of Jesus as they were in his genealogy, birth, and ministry. Their faithfulness was apparent in every phase of the ministry of Jesus—even to what seemed to many to be the end of his influence.

After three years of healings, miracles, and teachings, the earthly ministry of Jesus seemed to end in disaster for the twelve disciples. They had left everything to follow him, and then tragedy and catastrophe struck. Impetuous Peter proclaimed that he would ever deny the Lord, but soon afterward he did so three times. The other eleven men said the same thing. During Jesus's darkest moments in Gethsemane, they fell asleep. Judas betrayed the Lord and then later hanged himself. When Jesus was arrested, we read that all the disciples deserted him and fled (Matthew 26:56). Things were pretty much the same after the crucifixion. They cowered behind locked doors for fear of the Jews (John 20:19). And why not? If the Jews killed Jesus, they might just as easily kill his disciples, too. Even at the Great Commission some of the eleven doubted his resurrection (Matthew 28:17).

The gospels paint a different portrait of the many women who followed Jesus and supported him out of their personal means. These women traveled with and supported Jesus and his followers for nearly three years, witnessed Jesus's crucifixion, and then were the first heralds of the resurrection.

Mark writes that, at Jesus's death, "some women were watching from a distance. Among them were Mary Magdalene, Mary the mother of James the younger and of Joses, and Salome. In Galilee these women had followed him and cared for his needs. Many other women who had come up with him to Jerusalem were also there" (Mark 15:41).

Women were the last at the cross and the first at the tomb. Mark writes that when these women discovered the empty tomb, they trembled with bewilderment. "They said nothing to anyone, because they were afraid" (Mark 16:8). Matthew writes that they were "afraid yet filled with joy" (Matthew 28:8). When the women did tell the 11 men and the others about Jesus's resurrection, "they did not believe the women, because their words seemed to them like nonsense" (Luke 24:11). Thomas remained adamant in his doubts (John 20:24–25).

Two other men were walking to the village of Emmaus, downcast because of the violent end to all their dreams, when Jesus appeared to them. Jesus, whose identity remained hidden to them, asked what had happened, at which point Luke adds a delicious detail: "'Our women amazed us'" (Luke 24:22), they told Jesus, by declaring that Jesus was alive.

And finally, after the ascension, "the women"—as if their identities would have been obvious to the original readers—are also mentioned as part of the core disciples in the "upper room" (Acts 1:14).

Women in God's Service Today

If we fast-forward to the present day, we observe how women, some of them prominent and some of them unlikely, are playing an essential role in what God is doing in the world today. Consider Nobel laureate Leymah Gbowee, who tells her own story in her memoir *Mighty Be Our Powers: How Sisterhood, Prayer, and Sex Changed a Nation at War*. Gbowee observes in her preface that war is made by men and analyzed by men. Women are dismissed as a sidebar, marginalized like victims. Gbowee's own life and this book obliterate that misleading assumption.

Gbowee's book begins with her high school graduation party in 1989, when she is 17; six months later Liberia descends into fourteen years of savage civil war. In the first phase of the conflict (1989–1996), Charles Taylor and Prince Johnson overthrow the government of Samuel Doe, recording the grisly execution of Doe on an infamous videotape that later sells in Monrovia's marketplaces. Taylor is elected president in 1997, but two years later other forces oust him. By some estimates, 10 percent of the population is killed. Twenty-five percent flee the country. Starvation, systematic rape, torture, mutilation, and Taylor's cocaine-crazed child soldiers who wear outlandish costumes are what most people remember. Schools and hospitals close. Rats and dogs eat the unburied dead who litter the streets. There is no water, electricity, or phone service.

Gbowee's personal life mirrors the political chaos. Estranged from her parents, by the time she is 26 Gbowee has four children and no husband, education, income, or skills. She is trapped in a cruel cycle of depression and self-hatred due to domestic violence. She's on a slippery slope to Nowheresville. A turning point occurs in 1998, when Gbowee volunteers with the Trauma, Healing, and Reconciliation Program of the Lutheran Church and witnesses the "full horror of the war" in rural Liberia.

As Gbowee makes connections, her passion, hard work, and leadership skills emerge. One night she has a dream while sleeping on her office floor: "I didn't know where I was. Everything was dark. I couldn't see a face, but I heard a voice, and it was talking to me, commanding me: 'Gather the women to pray for peace!'" At 5 a.m. she wakes up shaking, feeling as though she has heard the voice of God.

Later that morning, Gbowee relates her dream to the women at her Lutheran church. Sister Esther Musah, an evangelist, leads them in prayer: "Dear God, thank you for sending us this vision. Give us your blessing, Lord, and offer us your protection and guidance in helping us to understand what it means." What it means is the start of the Liberian women's peace movement that ends the civil war.

About twenty Lutheran women begin to gather every Tuesday at noon to pray. Sometimes they fast. They invite other Christian churches. At one meeting Asatu speaks up: "I'm the only Muslim here, and we want to join this peace movement." "Praise the Lord!" shout the Christian women. And so Muslim and Christian women form an alliance. They share their horror stories. Training sessions and workshops follow. They pass out brochures and march to city hall. Three days a week for six months, they visit the mosques, the markets, and the churches of Monrovia: "Liberian women, awake for peace!" They stand by the thousands in the fish market every day in their trademark white T-shirts, in scorching sun and torrential rains. They announce "sex strikes" to all the men until the violence ceases. They picket the American Embassy. They demand peace.

In one especially moving encounter, shown in the film *Pray the Devil Back to Hell* (2008), Gbowee faces down the warlord–president Charles Taylor in a public ceremony: "We are tired of war! Tired of running! Tired of begging for wheat! Tired of our children being raped!"

In the end, the women force Charles Taylor to peace talks in Ghana, and then in Ghana they barricade the do-nothing-men in their plenary hall until they sign peace accords. After the 2003 accords, they are instrumental in disarming the country, registering voters, and electing Ellen Johnson Sirleaf as the first woman head of state in Africa.

Who are these Liberian women? "I will say," says Gbowee, "they are ordinary mothers, grandmothers, aunts, sisters." They sowed bitter tears. They went out weeping. They followed in the tradition of the stories in both the Old and New Testaments of the central role of women in redemption. And they acted on their dreams of peace, joy, and laughter for their beloved nation.

The Story Continues

These biblical stories (and we could mention many more) demonstrate how God has elevated women to prominent roles in the story of redemption. Many of these women are the types of people that society tends to marginalize: the poor, the widow, the alien, and an unwed teenager like Mary. Today we would rightly include those with HIV. The people of God depend on them today, just as they did in biblical times, to hear the call of God, to lift up their voices, and to lead us on the journey with Jesus.

Additional Reading

Gbowee, Leymah, with Carol Mithers. *Mighty Be Our Powers: How Sisterhood, Prayer, and Sex Changed a Nation at War: A Memoir*. New York: Beast Books, 2011.

Phiri, Isabel Apawo, and Sarojini Nadar, editors. *African Women, Religion, and Health: Essays in Honor of Mercy Amba Ewudziwa Oduyoye*. Maryknoll, NY: Orbis, 2006.

Sayers, Dorothy. *Are Women Human?* Grand Rapids: Eerdmans, 2005.

———. *Unpopular Opinions: Twenty-one Essays*. New York: Harcourt, Brace, 1947.

5

A Biblical Case for the Value and Dignity of Women

SHARON GALLAGHER

Introduction

THE HIV EPIDEMIC WAS first described in 1981. When it began, 95% of those infected were men. Over the next decade, the number of infected women increased at a more rapid rate than that of men, reaching over 50% of those infected worldwide. In Sub-Saharan Africa, 60% of people living with HIV are women. Although there are biological reasons why women are more susceptible to HIV per sexual act, it's clear that the increasing number of women with HIV is also related to political, social, economic, and educational factors. A common denominator for these issues is that women have little to no power to protect themselves from unwanted sex, or even physical or sexual violence. So, a theological understanding of the increasing number of women infected with HIV, and the discrimination that follows, is that HIV infection is a consequence of violating the dignity of women that is established and promoted in the Scriptures.

In response to the discrimination and marginalization facing women with HIV, we people of faith ask what the Scriptures tell us about the status of women. We'll start by looking at the biblical account of human origins.

It's hard to overemphasize the importance of the Genesis account of the creation of man and woman. This chronicle has affected the way three of the major world religions view women and, primarily through the influence of Christianity and Judaism, has shaped the way all of Western civilization perceives women.

Beginnings

In the early chapters of Genesis, we're told that humans were created to live in fellowship with God and with one another: "Then God said, 'Let us make man in our image, in our likeness, and let them rule over the fish of the sea and the birds of the air, over the livestock, over all the earth, and over all the creatures that move along the ground.' So God created man in his own image, in the image of God he created him; male and female he created them" (Genesis 1:26–27).

These verses are packed with meaning. We learn that both male and female are made in God's image, which immediately conveys an enormous sense of dignity and worth to both sexes. It's also clear that the relationship between man and woman mirrors the relationship of the Trinity: Our fellowship is a reflection of God's own nature. We also see that dominion and stewardship over the created world were given to both men and women. There is no sense in this early part of the story that man had dominion over woman.

In Genesis 1:31 we're told that, "God saw all that he had made, and it was very good." Male and female were "good." In this first account, man and woman were created at the same time, and both "in God's image."

In the second creation account (Genesis 2), man was created first, which some interpret as implying superiority. But God decided that it was not good for the man to be alone (by himself, he's not so "good") and created the woman as a helper for him. Man became complete with the creation of woman.

The word translated "helper" has sometimes given the impression that the woman was created in a secondary position, as the man's assistant or housekeeper. But nowhere in the Bible is this word used to designate a subordinate. In fact, there are passages where it's used to describe God. For example, in Psalms 146:5, we are told that "Blessed is he whose help is the God of Jacob." In this second account, the emphasis is on sameness. Unlike the rest of the animal kingdom, the woman was the same kind of being as the man. Adam acknowledged this when he said, "This is now bone of my bones and flesh of my flesh; she shall be called 'woman,' for she was taken out of man" (Genesis 2:23).

In the third chapter of Genesis, everything changed. The perfect harmony men and women were created to live in with God, with each other, and with the rest of the created world was broken. After the fall, the lives of men and women would be different. But this was not a curse; it was a prediction of what would happen when sin entered the world. The domination and subjugation of women were not what God intended but were a result of the fall, and the fall is not the last word.

The whole history of God's relationship with humanity is an invitation to live beyond the fall, entering into a restored harmony with God and with each other. Even in God's harsh words to the serpent, there's a promise of redemption: "And I will put enmity between you and the woman, and between your offspring and hers; he will crush your head, and you will strike his heel" (Genesis 3:15).

There is a long history of interpreting that verse as a messianic prophesy—meaning that, although Jesus was wounded on the cross, ultimately, evil will be crushed by what Jesus accomplished on the cross. The name *Eve* means "Mother of All Living," and there is great hope in that name. Not only is the meaning of *Eve* true in the sense that Eve is the mother of generations of humanity, but also in the sense that, through her line, another woman will give birth to the one who gives us all life.

Hebrew Scriptures reflect the patriarchal society of the ancient Middle East. But because God continued to work in the life of Israel, there are many surprising stories of female leaders who became important figures in Jewish history. We hear about Miriam, who rescued Moses; Esther, who saved the nation; Ruth, who chose the God of Israel; and Deborah, a military leader, judge, prophetess, and poet.

It's remarkable to read about these women. Their stories reveal that, though Israel instituted a male monarchy, God continued to work through men and women chosen for their great faith. Some of these women are honored not only in Hebrew scriptures but in the first pages of the New Testament.

Matthew's Genealogy

Matthew begins his gospel with a genealogy showing that Jesus was a descendent of David—fulfilling messianic prophesy. But the list has several surprises, starting with the inclusion of women. Since women were of low status and considered of little importance, it's extraordinary that they're on a list meant to establish the royal lineage. That they are named in this genealogy shows that women, as well as men, have been part of God's salvation history leading up to the birth of the promised Messiah.

Another surprise is who these women were. At least two of them, Ruth and Rahab, were not Israelites. Matthew's inclusion of them tells us that redemptive history includes people not ethnically Jewish, and that the birth of Jesus will benefit all of humanity.

Several of the women on the list have questionable sexual histories. Rahab had been a prostitute, and Bathsheba an adulteress. Matthew doesn't mention Bathsheba by name but refers to her as the wife, not of David, but of Uriah—a pointed reminder of the adultery involved in the union that produced Solomon, part of the kingly line.

In the situation of David and Bathsheba, all the power belonged to David: Bathsheba could not have refused the king. David decided to sleep with Bathsheba. When she became pregnant, he contrived to have her husband killed in battle. Some suggest that Bathsheba shared in the blame for David's actions, but this is not the biblical view. When the prophet Nathan confronted David about his sin, no blame was cast on Bathsheba. In Nathan's parable about a man with many lambs who takes the only lamb of a poor man, Uriah is the poor man, Bathsheba is the innocent lamb, and David is the sinner. In God's eyes, David is responsible for his own lustful acts.

Yet, even knowing all this, when I reread the genealogy, the inclusion of Bathsheba is always a little surprising, while the inclusion of David, also an adulterer, is not. I've been conditioned to expect women to be judged differently than men. The way Matthew writes the genealogy forces us to see things differently.

Women are included in the genealogical records of the line that ran from Eve to Mary, moving toward the birth of the Messiah and the ultimate redemption of both men and women. This inclusion of women on the list points to our being born again in Christ, a rebirth which includes redemption of the relationships between men and women. The best guide for what this redemption might look like is in the example of Jesus and the surprising ways that he interacted with and affirmed women.

The Woman Caught in Adultery

In Jesus's day, compared to men, women had limited control over their lives. And, from the following account in John 8:3–11, it seems that there was a deep sexual double standard in Jesus's day, as there is in our own: "The teachers of the law and the Pharisees brought in a woman caught in adultery. They made her stand before the group and said to Jesus, 'Teacher, this woman was caught in the act of adultery. In the Law Moses commanded us to stone such women. Now what do you say?' They were using this question as a trap, in order to have a basis for accusing him.

But Jesus bent down and started to write on the ground with his finger. When they kept on questioning him, he straightened up and said to them, 'Let any one of you who is without sin be the first to throw a stone at her.' Again he stooped down and wrote on the ground.

At this, those who heard began to go away one at a time, the older ones first, until only Jesus was left, with the woman still standing there. Jesus straightened up and asked her, 'Woman, where are they? Has no one condemned you?' 'No one, sir,' she said. 'Then neither do I condemn you,' Jesus declared. 'Go now and leave your life of sin.'"

The first thing we might notice is that there's a missing male: Only one party stands accused here. Clearly the woman had a partner, and yet she alone is confronted. We might also wonder what Jesus wrote on the ground; there are many theories about this. One of them is that Jesus was writing down the secret sins of the men watching. We do know from verse 7 that Jesus turned the double-standard back on those who accused this woman. The way Jesus responds to her accusers reminds them that they, too, are sinners and that this woman is not defined by her sin. Jesus's interest is not in her condemnation but in her redemption. Kenneth E. Bailey comments: "The Pharisees want strict application of the law. Jesus fights for compassion for the bruised reed and the dimly burning wick that he sees in the woman before him" (quoting Isaiah 42:3).

Jesus, as always, sees beyond "the law" to the person—weak, shamed, and in danger of a death sentence. The Pharisees want the law applied, but only to her, to the woman. The commandment "You shall not commit adultery" was given to both men and women, yet they seem completely unconcerned about the man with whom they must have "caught" her. They are not forming a vigilante group to hunt this culprit down. Their sense of justice is warped, and they are far from the even higher standard of compassion that Jesus embodies.

Two Stories

Here are two stories about women with an illness that caused them to be excluded from their communities—and one that was transformed by the compassion of Jesus.

The first story was told in a movie made in South Africa. It's not a true story, but it's based on countless stories of women for whom this has been a reality. The movie introduces us to a lovely young woman named Yesterday. Her husband is away working in mines for months at a time, and, though she misses him, she stays on their small property, tending the garden and taking loving care of their daughter, Beauty. But Yesterday hasn't been feeling well, and the town's new schoolteacher advises her to see a doctor. Yesterday gets up early and waits in long lines at a clinic only to be turned away, repeatedly, because the day's quota of patients has been met. When she is finally seen by a physician, she is diagnosed as infected with HIV and is told that she should let her husband know, as he is likely infected as well.

Since she can't reach her husband by phone, she takes a bus to Johannesburg. When she tells her husband that she has the disease, which means that he also is infected with HIV, and in fact has given it to her, he beats her mercilessly.

Yesterday goes back to the village, where she struggles to perform daily chores as she grows weaker and weaker. When her husband returns home to die, she cares for him as well. The village women, realizing that he has HIV and she may, too, shun her, making her life even more desolate.

The second story is true and happened centuries before in Israel. It is told in Luke 8:41–48. It's the story of a woman with an issue of blood who touches Jesus. In that society, women were not allowed to touch men, and a woman who was hemorrhaging would have been considered unclean. The *Encyclopaedia Judaica* says that a menstruating woman is in a state of ritual impurity that "is considered hateful to God, and man is to take care in order not to find himself thus excluded from His divine presence." But this woman was desperate and touched Jesus anyway. When Jesus asked who touched him, she answered that it was she, trembling with fear at the audacity of what she had done. But instead of rebuking her, Jesus healed her and commended her for her faith.

This woman's illness had destroyed her health and depleted all her financial resources. In addition, the nature of her illness—the fact that she was unclean—cut her off from human society. She had to bear all of her problems in isolation from community, until Jesus healed her. Her health restored her to human society; her faith restored her spiritually; and Jesus called her "daughter," welcoming her to the family of God.

During his ministry, Jesus made it clear that sick people were not being punished for their sins, or the sins of their parents. We're all sinners, and all of our parents were sinners. Unlike us, Jesus was truly holy, yet he responded to this hemorrhaging woman, not as a woman, not as someone "unclean," but as someone with great faith, whose faith was rewarded.

When sick people approached Jesus, he did not stop to determine whether or not they were responsible for their illness, or whether they were worthy or unworthy of healing. What interested Jesus was the person's faith. In the same way, we're not asked to determine who the worthy or unworthy poor are or who the worthy and unworthy sick are; we're just told to help them.

The Apostle Paul and Women

When we read the Gospel accounts, it's clear that Jesus was a great friend to women. As Dorothy L. Sayers wrote in her wonderful essay "Are Women Human?": "Perhaps it is no wonder that the women were first at the Cradle and last at the Cross. They had never known a man like this Man—there never had been such another, a prophet and teacher who never nagged at them, never flattered or coaxed or patronized . . ."

But as we leave the Gospels and read further in the New Testament, the Pauline passages about women's roles appear to be more restrictive, at least in the ways they've been translated and interpreted. To understand what the great apostle was really saying, we need to read his words about women with great care.

First of all, we should remember that Paul was a follower of Jesus, and we can assume that he didn't contradict what he learned from the example of Jesus.

Paul was faced with the tough job of helping the fledgling churches apply their new faith, a faith that was freeing for both men and women, in a restrictive Middle Eastern context. As we read Paul's letters to these churches, we need to distinguish between the overarching principles for all Christians and the problems addressed to individual churches in a specific culture. For example, Paul told women to have their heads covered when they were praying and prophesying. In that culture, for a woman to have her head uncovered often meant that she was a prostitute or an immoral wife. (In our Western culture, it does not mean that.)

Clearly, since this was a problem Paul addressed, women who understood their new freedom in Christ were throwing off their old restrictions. But Paul wanted Christians to live peaceably with their neighbors without making Christianity a cause for scandal, except for the great scandal of the cross.

An example of Paul's teaching that is clearly for all Christians is the great text found in Galatians 3:28: "There is neither Jew nor Greek, slave nor free, male nor female, for you are all one in Christ Jesus." Interestingly, the NIV Bible captions this passage on emancipation and equality, sometimes called the "Magna Carta" for women, "Sons of God." Eugene Peterson in *The Message* more appropriately captions the same section "In Christ's Family."

This brings us to another consideration. Although the Bible is the inspired word of God, translators are human beings who often bring their biases to the text. For example, in 1 Timothy 2:11 the word translated "silence" in the King James Version is translated as "quiet" in the NIV. "Let a woman learn in silence with full submission." There's a great deal of difference between worshiping quietly and being silent. This decision by translators influenced church practice for generations, silencing the voices and limiting the gifts of many Christian women. A woman should learn in quietness and full submission.

But newer translations aren't always better. In 1 Timothy 2:12, the King James Version tells us that women are not to "usurp" authority over men, indicating that the problem is about their way of taking authority (which is close to the meaning of the original Greek word). But some modern translations such as the NIV say "I do not permit a woman to teach or to have authority over a man; she must be silent."

New Testament scholar N. T. Wright helpfully summarizes the meaning of 1 Timothy 2:8–15: "On the one hand women should be trained and educated in the faith (in contrast to much of the Roman empire), but on the other hand Christianity should not become a cult like that of Artemis in Ephesus, where women did the leading and kept the men in line. Men should not lord it over women, nor women over men."

One way of understanding what Paul meant and how his admonitions were understood in their original context is to look at early church practice. The fact that Paul asked women to pray and prophesy with their heads covered, for example, indicates that they *were* participating in public worship rather sitting there as "silent" onlookers.

In Romans 16:1–16, where Paul lists his notable associates, among the twenty-nine people mentioned, ten are women. Paul Jewett comments that this listing is a magnificent affirmation that the phrase "There is neither Jew nor Greek, slave nor free, male nor female, for you are all one in Christ Jesus" was not merely a matter of theory for Paul. Yet, even in this remarkable list we find biases of translation.

In the King James Version, Romans 16:1 reads, "I commend to you Phoebe our sister who is a *servant* of the church which is at Cenchrea." Elsewhere, when applied to men, the same word for "servant" is translated "deacon" or "minister." S. Scott Bartchy has commented that, while it's not wrong to translate that word "servant," it's very wrong to only translate it as "servant" for a woman, while giving the title "deacon" for a man.

Another argument used to limit the role of women is found in Ephesians 5:22, which says "Wives, submit to your husbands." For years the only verse in this passage I ever heard quoted in sermons was this one about a woman submitting to her husband. The preceding verse was never mentioned, and in many translations it's separated from the rest of passage by a heading (such as "Wives and Husbands" in the NIV). But Ephesians 5:21 begins the discussion about relationships between spouses with an overriding principle for all believers: "Submit to one another out of reverence for Christ." This puts the rest of the passage in perspective. Christians, both men and women, are to submit themselves one to another. Ignoring the way Paul introduces the passage does real violence to its meaning.

In *The Message*, Eugene Peterson, appropriately, titles the passage "Relationships" and begins with verse 21, with its emphasis on mutuality. The passage goes on in verse 25 to tell men: "Husbands, love your wives, just as Christ loved the church and gave himself up for her . . ." In that ancient Middle Eastern culture, as in many cultures today, men had all the power. When Paul tells them to behave as Christ did toward the church, he doesn't talk about Christ the King, the Lord of all creation. Men are exhorted to love their wives as Christ loved the church—sacrificing himself for her. They're challenged to follow Christ as the suffering servant who gave himself for us.

In verse 28, men are told to love their wives as themselves: "In this same way, husbands ought to love their wives as their own bodies. He who loves his wife loves himself." This is a statement about the mystical unity in marriage. This reminder that husbands and wives are "of the same flesh" calls for restoration of the harmony that men and women lost because of the fall.

When these Pauline passages are read with care, it becomes clear that Paul is following Jesus in being a great friend to women.

Following Jesus

On a recent mission trip to Cambodia, my cousin and his wife met a woman with a beautiful but very sad face. As they got to know her better, she shared her story with them—a story illustrating that the failure to view young girls and women with the dignity that Jesus taught can lead to sexual exploitation. Some years before, a man came through their village and offered to put her daughter into a good school. The woman allowed her daughter to leave with the man and has never heard from her since. The young girl was probably forced into child prostitution, quite possibly in Bangkok, Thailand, where many of the city's over 400,000 prostitutes come from Cambodia (an even poorer country than Thailand). This in itself is a tragic story, the child cut off from her mother by a false promise of a better life. But the other reality is that life as a sex worker will put her daughter at high risk for HIV infection: Her "kidnapping" may also be a death sentence.

Some years ago, a young woman from my church went to Thailand as a missionary. As she ministered there, she saw many bar girls and street prostitutes become Christians. But within a short time these women were back on the streets, because they had no other means of support. My friend's response was to start a crafts collective where women could earn money, making items for sale in the U.S. This was a creative response based on the realities these women faced and showed the compassion of Jesus for their physical as well as spiritual well-being.

In the Old Testament, the prophet Isaiah calls God's people to "defend the cause of the fatherless, plead the case of the widow" (Isaiah 1:17). Jesus told his disciples that those who truly knew him would take care of those who were strangers, poor, hungry, sick, or in prison—"the least of these" (Matthew 25:31–46). In his epistle, the apostle James encouraged the young Christian churches to care for their widows and orphans, saying that this is religion that God accepts as "pure and faultless" (James 1:27). It's clear from the book of Acts that the early Church was concerned about widows and the poor and was willing to share its resources. The AIDS epidemic has left many widows and orphans in its wake. The Church today, like the early Church, is called to respond with practical help.

Conclusion

We know that Jesus is no longer physically present in our gritty, sinful, un-just world, healing and forgiving the sick, the sinful, the marginalized, and the powerless. But the Church—"the body of Christ"—and we—members of that body—are still present in the world. We can show those who are sick the compassion that Jesus showed. We can value women the way Jesus did.

Those who emphasize the sinfulness of humanity in the first chapters of Genesis tend to limit the roles of women in church and society. Those who emphasize redemption see women as made in the image of God and as coheirs of salvation. Let's live in light of the redemption, not in bondage to the fall.

Additional Reading

Bailey, Kenneth E. *Jesus through Middle Eastern Eyes: Cultural Studies in the Gospels.* Downers Grove, IL: InterVarsity, 2008.

Kroeger, Catherine C., and Mary J. Evans, editors. *Women's Bible Commentary* Downers Grove, IL: InterVarsity, 2002.

Kroeger, Catherine C., and Richard C. Kroeger. *I Suffer Not a Woman: Rethinking I Timothy 2:11–15 in Light of Ancient Evidence.* Grand Rapids: Baker, 1992.

Wright, N. T. *1 & 2 Timothy and Titus: 12 Studies for Individuals and Groups.* Downers Grove, IL: InterVarsity, 2009.

6

The Feminization of the HIV Epidemic

ARTHUR J. AMMANN

Then Mary took about a pint of pure nard, an expensive perfume; she poured it on Jesus' feet and wiped his feet with her hair. And the house was filled with the fragrance of the perfume. But one of his disciples, Judas Iscariot, who was later to betray him, objected, "Why wasn't this perfume sold and the money given to the poor? It was worth a year's wages." He did not say this because he cared about the poor but because he was a thief; as keeper of the money bag, he used to help himself to what was put into it. "Leave her alone," Jesus replied. "[It was intended] that she should save this perfume for the day of my burial. You will always have the poor among you, but you will not always have me." (John 12:3–8)

WORLDWIDE, THERE ARE NOW more women infected with HIV than men— a trend that will continue indefinitely unless more effective ways are found to prevent women from becoming infected. The shift from a predominance of men to a predominance of women being affected in the global HIV epidemic also has significant consequences for children. In most cultures, women are the mainstay of family support and stability. All over the world, untreated HIV is robbing mothers of their health and their very lives—and their children are left without the care that these mothers once provided. The loss of a mother's ability to care for her family through illness or death then creates a secondary epidemic—one of orphaned children. The number of children orphaned by the HIV epidemic currently exceeds 16 million, with 5 to 6 million new orphans added each year. Soon this number will exceed the total number of individuals with HIV worldwide.

Research and clinical studies in HIV have produced some of the most remarkable advances in the history of medicine. We know more about the human immunodeficiency virus (HIV), the cause of AIDS, than any other virus. We have more than 30 drugs and combinations of drugs to treat HIV—more than any other viral infection. We know how to prevent every means of HIV transmission. Yet, in spite of all of our knowledge, we are failing to control the relentless increase in infections that now accounts for 3 million new infections each year—with over 50% of these occurring in women. Once someone is infected with HIV, the virus remains active even with treatment. Lifelong HIV infection and the potential for concomitant lifelong HIV transmission accounts for the continued cumulative escalation of the epidemic to its present level of 30 million individuals living with HIV.

The term "feminization" of HIV is used to describe the shift of the epidemic from a majority of men in the 1980s to a majority of women and young girls beginning in 2001. In the U.S., individuals aged 13 to 24 account for 50% of the over 40,000 new infections each year. The majority of the 15 million women who are HIV-infected worldwide are of childbearing age. Approximately 2 million women who have HIV become pregnant each year, which contributes to the dramatic increase in the estimated 6 million children orphaned and left vulnerable due to HIV. The HIV epidemic in women is most severe in Sub-Saharan Africa, where as many as 65% of infections are in women. In many countries, the ratio of young girls to young boys infected with HIV exceeds 4 to 1. Biological, sociological/cultural, political/legal, behavioral, economic, and religious factors converge to enhance a woman's susceptibility to HIV.

For each sexual act, an uninfected woman is eight times more likely to become infected from an infected man than an uninfected man is from an infected woman. This enhanced susceptibility is postulated to be a consequence of the large surface area of the vagina and the presence of other sexually transmitted infections. Young girls are at greater risk than older women. The vaginal epithelium of a young girl is thinner, and the cervix is composed of a single layer of columnar epithelium, which increases the potential for HIV infection—as compared to an older woman, who has a thicker vaginal epithelium and a cervix composed of multiple layers of squamous epithelium.

Cultural and religious practices and theological interpretations of Old Testament and New Testament Scriptures are contributing to increased rates of HIV infection in women. The Old Testament practice of wife inheritance by brothers following the death of a husband increases the potential of introducing HIV into a subsequent marital relationship. The theological interpretation of Scripture that women are to be subservient to men contributes to women's lack of choice in their sexual relationships, meaning that sometimes their only choice is to marry a man infected with HIV and risk unprotected sexual relations. Increased HIV infection of women from HIV-infected men results from refusal of men, on theological or other grounds, to use condoms—even though HIV infection is usually caused by unprotected sex. The practice of polygamy among some Muslim and Christian groups contributes to the spread of HIV to multiple sexual partners.

Cultural practices also contribute to increased risk of HIV infection for women. In some African cultures the ritual of "sexual cleansing" following the death of a husband, a widow is required to have sexual relations with male relatives to "cleanse" her from the spirit of her dead husband. Several cultures and religions encourage early marriage of young girls. Frequently the husband is an older man who is sexually experienced and HIV-infected. Sex outside of marriage and extramarital sex during pregnancy are additional factors that contribute to a higher rate of HIV infection in women than men.

Male dominance over sexual decisions prevents women from protecting themselves from HIV infection. If a woman refuses to have sex or asks that a condom be used, she is often subjected to sexual and physical abuse. Intimate partner violence is one of the major associations linked to HIV infection of women. Advocates for women have demanded the development of female-controlled methods for protection against sexually transmitted infections and HIV. A female-controlled microbicide that could prevent just 50% of HIV infections in women could save the lives of more than 1 million women each year and prevent the orphanhood of millions of children.

Poverty also contributes to the increased number of women who are infected with HIV. Families may sell their young girls into prostitution in order to obtain money for basic necessities. The rate of HIV infection among prostitutes is up to 10 times greater than women in the general population. When women or young girls become HIV-infected, they are no longer profitable to the sex industry. They are dismissed and return to their homes, only to be rejected because of their HIV infection and their need for health care and support. In politically unstable and extremely impoverished regions of the world, young girls and women are taken advantage of by "sugar daddies" who provide them with food or minimal sums of money in return for unprotected sex. Within the sex trade industry, a higher premium is paid for sex without a condom or with a young virgin girl. The economic plight of women and young girls throughout the world perpetuates the use of sex as a means of immediate survival while increasing the risk of long-term disease and death from HIV.

Putting aside for a moment the incalculable physical, emotional, and spiritual costs of the HIV infection of women, the economic costs alone of HIV infection are staggering. The cost of treatment to keep 10 million or more women with HIV healthy and productive runs into billions of dollars each year. As most HIV-infected women eventually die or become too sick to care for their children, the responsibility of care and education for children who become orphaned and who are left vulnerable increases costs dramatically, adding even more billions of dollars. Of course, it is not only the economic costs of HIV that should be of concern. Women as a whole provide family and community stability. They are generally caregivers, educators, sustainers, peacemakers, and providers of the love and care that nurture the future generations. The stigma of HIV results in physical and emotional isolation, which, in turn, removes women who have HIV from desperately needed social, community, and spiritual support.

Political and legal injustices create an atmosphere of indifference and permissiveness toward the sexual abuse of women and toward women's lack of control over sexual decisions. In many instances, the police benefit financially from the sex trade or are given "free" sex in return for ignoring sex trafficking in women and young girls. There has also been a reluctance to accept the customary purposefulness of sexual abuse and rape during times of conflict and to equate it with a form of genocide. Yet, behind the deliberate rape of a woman is the intent to render her stigmatized and "useless" to her husband, family, and community. Rape by an HIV-infected soldier is an insidious means of planting "viral landmines" that will have their rampant impact long after armed conflict has ceased.

International public health communities may also contribute to the expansion of the HIV epidemic in women by failing to fully implement traditional measures to control sexually transmitted infections such as HIV. The standard for controlling sexually transmitted diseases is to perform routine diagnostic testing, partner notification, and contact tracing. In resource-poor countries, men access antiretroviral drug treatment (drugs that treat HIV) more readily than women. Additionally, many international public health programs do not require that a man infected with HIV notify his partner or identify other sexual partners who might be at risk for HIV infection. Now that lifesaving treatment is available, it is not medically or ethically justifiable to treat one sexual partner and leave undiagnosed and untreated the other sexual partner.

The many injustices and inequities directed toward women, resulting in the feminization of the HIV epidemic, have acted synergistically to transform what was initially an infectious disease epidemic into a simultaneous and parallel epidemic of human rights abuse of women. A woman's right to not have sex or to not become pregnant has long been an issue. Also at issue is the right to not become infected with a lethal virus such as HIV. Tragically, no country or culture seems to be immune to the destructive forces that effect these cataclysms.

The paradox of the ever-expanding HIV epidemic is that successful methods for reducing or preventing HIV transmission in women are available—for every means of transmission. Individuals who abstain from sex, who are faithful to a single sexual partner, or who use condoms rarely will, if ever, become infected. Testing of blood donors substantially reduces the risk of blood-transfusion HIV. Treatment of a pregnant woman who has HIV with antiretroviral drugs greatly reduces the potential for HIV transmission to her baby during gestation and delivery, and substitution of formula feeding for breast-feeding eliminates breast milk HIV transmission. Needle- and syringe-exchange programs are effective for reducing HIV risk among intravenous drug users.

The HIV epidemic has thrown the spotlight on the unequal protection of women. As long as women remain devalued in our societies, the HIV epidemic will persist as one predominately of women, as well as an increasing number of orphans and vulnerable children. Old Testament and New Testament injunctions to honor and protect women, especially widows and those who are disadvantaged, stand in stark contrast to what has happened to women in every country affected by the HIV epidemic. As Christians, we must address the reasons that discrimination and stigmatization of women is so persistent and exaggerated in relation to HIV, in spite of pervasive Judeo-Christian ethics.

The teachings of Jesus are able to radically change the current feminization of the HIV epidemic. The Gospels are replete with examples of the respect that Jesus had for women, regardless of their status. Women were an integral part of his ministry, and he particularly defended those who were at the point of being condemned by political and religious leaders.

"The teachers of the law and the Pharisees brought in a woman caught in adultery. They made her stand before the group and said to Jesus, 'Teacher, this woman was caught in the act of adultery. In the Law Moses commanded us to stone such women. Now what do you say?' They were using this question as a trap, in order to have a basis for accusing him. But Jesus bent down and started to write on the ground with his finger.

When they kept on questioning him, he straightened up and said to them, 'If any one of you is without sin, let him be the first to throw a stone at her.'

Again he stooped down and wrote on the ground. At this, those who heard began to go away one at a time, the older ones first, until only Jesus was left, with the woman still standing there. Jesus straightened up and asked her, 'Woman, where are they? Has no one condemned you?'

'No one, sir,' she said. 'Then neither do I condemn you,' Jesus declared. 'Go now and leave your life of sin.'" (John 8:3–11)

The challenge for the Christian is whether we have the courage of Jesus to love, to understand, and to discern what spiritual truth is when we are faced with a person with a disease that may be foreign to us: How do our beliefs translate into action in light of the injustices and inequities that relate to the feminization of the HIV epidemic? We are taught through our Judeo-Christian heritage to respond to all who are suffering—those who are poor, those from other countries, and especially those who have been widowed and orphaned. It is impossible to read through the Old and New Testaments without concluding that God has always been most interested in the disadvantaged: refugees, widows, orphans, and other people left vulnerable. We can safely deduce that God sees these individuals as deserving of unique and passionate protection.

I believe that there are times of desperate need, both physical and spiritual, that Christians ignore because we do not see them as Jesus sees them. This is true in regards to the AIDS epidemic. The Church in America has lived outside the community of pain and suffering induced by this disease. The arm of those who suffer from HIV has been severed from the body of Christ, and in "amputating" this arm of suffering, the Christian Church has missed the blessing that comes from living out the teachings of Jesus regarding those who are poor and needy.

The words of Jesus are simple and unambiguous: We are to care for people who are needy, suffering, widowed, and orphaned. Jesus does not introduce a qualifier as to the cause of the suffering in order for us to respond. It is blatant that Jesus's ministry to the disadvantaged, outcasts, women, and those with infirmities—all of whom were shunned by the established religious leaders—provide us with precise examples of how we should act.

For Christians worldwide, the HIV epidemic is a test of how deeply we believe in God's mercy and justice and in the teachings of Jesus—how complete is our forgiveness, how rich is our compassion, and how far does our love reach out to overcome the stigmatization and discrimination of HIV to comfort those in pain and suffering. The Church continues to grapple with how to respond to the challenges of protecting women from HIV infection and defending and caring for those who are already infected. There remains an opportunity for the Christian community to distinguish itself by demonstrating how Jesus taught us to respond to those most in need.

Additional Reading

Patterson, Jacqui et al. *Together We Must End Violence against Women and Girls and HIV & AIDS: A Review of Promising Practices in Addressing the Intersection.* UNIFEM, United Nations Development Fund for Women, and ActionAid, 2009. Online: http://www.unifem.org/attachments/products/TogetherWeMust_en.pdf.

Phiri, Isabel Apawo, and Sarojini Nadar, editors. *African Women, Religion, and Health: Essays in Honor of Mercy Amba Ewudziwa Oduyoye.* Maryknoll, NY: Orbis, 2006.

World Health Organization. (October 23–25, 2000). *Violence against Women and HIV/AIDS: Setting the Research Agenda.* Meeting Report. Geneva, Switzerland. Online: http://www.who.int/gender/violence/VAWhiv.pdf.

7

Theology of Care for the Vulnerable

DAVID W. GILL

Introduction: Not Many Mighty

OUR WORLD LOVES THE strong, the beautiful, the brilliant, the successful, and the rich. That's who you see in advertising, on the news, on the stage. We are surrounded by their images and trappings. We are supposed to admire them and want to be like them.

It is then a strange contrast to read St. Paul's famous words to the early Christian church: "Brothers and sisters, not many of you were wise by human standards; not many were influential; not many were of noble birth. But God chose the foolish things of the world . . . God chose the weak things of the world . . . God chose the lowly things of this world and the despised things" (1 Corinthians 1:26–28).

This hardly seems like a strategy for building a great movement throughout the world, as Christianity was to become. But it is the truth: Jesus Christ gravitated to the sick, to the hungry, to the outcast, and to those at the margins of society during his three years of public ministry. His was a ministry to the vulnerable of his time. He excluded no one—including women, who were excluded from the religious practices of the day. Throughout history, whenever the Christian church has been most alive, it has continued this tradition of valuing the presence and gifts of women. Whenever Christian leaders have forsaken the weak for the strong, the poor for the rich, the unknown for the popular, the movement has stagnated and lost its way.

In this chapter, I will review the biblical story of God's particular focus on the vulnerable: women (especially widows), children (especially orphans), the elderly (especially grandparents who may be called on to care for their orphaned grandchildren), the poor (especially those who have suffered economic loss because of HIV), the sick and injured (especially those who suffer from the disability of HIV infection), and the stranger (the political, national, racial, or religious "other," and especially those who are strangers because they are HIV-infected) and how each one of these relates to our response to the HIV epidemic. After reminding ourselves that God has a special concern for these populations, we will ask *why*. And more than just asking why God cares, we must ask why *we* should care for the vulnerable. The answer has to do with both compassion and justice. It has to do with the very real value that lies within the vulnerable and victimized persons themselves. It has to do with God and our relationship to him. And, finally, it has to do with who we are, with our own humanity and character.

Vulnerability is defined as "susceptibility to emotional and physical injury; susceptibility to attack and/or subject to harm." Understanding how vulnerability comes about and who is most susceptible is key to understanding both why women are uniquely susceptible to the forces that produce it and why Jesus paid particular attention to women in general, and to vulnerable women in particular.

The Women

To be sure, there are women as powerful as any man could ever hope to be, fully able to defend themselves, win any argument, manage any complex situation, solve any problem, and lead any movement. It used to be a joke that British Prime Minister Margaret Thatcher was "the toughest man in Europe." Hillary Clinton and Condoleezza Rice are the equals of any American politician or diplomat in memory, whether one agrees with their policies or not. Examples of female strength, power, and achievement easily could be given from business, the arts, the professions, academia, and sports as well.

According to the Bible, man and woman, equally, are created in the image and likeness of God, blessed, commissioned in partnership to "be fruitful and increase in number; fill the earth and subdue it" (Genesis 1:27–28). Any differentiation and separation of their roles was a direct result of sin, not of the creational intention of God (Genesis 3). And in the great prophecy of Joel (2:28–29, cited in Acts 2:17), God says, "I will pour out my Spirit on all people. Your sons and daughters will prophesy . . ." Whatever differences in role and calling there may be between men and women in our history, these need to be understood as subordinate to the grand themes of Creation and Pentecost—looking back to God's beginning and looking forward to God's future. God continually surprises both his chosen people and the world by raising up leaders like Deborah; Esther; the virtuous multi-tasking businesswoman of Proverbs 31; the humble Mary, mother of our Lord; the female witnesses to the cross and the empty tomb; Lydia and Priscilla, prominent in the early Church.

Yet, apart from the apparent equality men and women possess in God's sight, there are distinct biological differences. In childbearing, women experience pain and risk that utterly escape men. In becoming pregnant and in feeding and nurturing her children, a mother usually has a vastly greater role than a father. Biological differences often translate into cultural and sociological differences. The way that women throughout the world typically nurture and care for others contrasts with the often brutal assaults, abuse, and rape inflicted by men—often by marauding, drunken men or militias—not just their enemies but sometimes even their own families. Too often, male selfishness refuses to take any steps to protect female victims from sexually transmitted diseases like HIV. Women are infected with HIV by men and left to suffer the often fatal consequences. They are humiliated and sometimes ostracized—often by male church leaders—not for their own choices, but for what was done to them by males.

Where are the Christian men who will stand up and protect these precious women? Where are the fathers and elders who will not only set a personal example of virtuous behavior toward women and girls, but also speak up and act decisively to protect them from attackers and abusers? Where are those who demand an end to violence against women?

HIV infection of women and sexual violence are closely linked. The most common form of violence against women is called intimate (domestic) partner violence: physical and/or sexual violence that occurs between sexual partners who are not casual partners but who know each other well. In some studies—for example, in South Africa—over 50% of women who have HIV infection have a history of intimate partner violence. Too many think that intimate partner violence results only in visible and immediate evidence of abuse: bruises, broken bones, or tissue trauma following forceful sexual intercourse. HIV infection that occurs at the time of sexual violence may not become evident, however, until years after infection. Many are now of the opinion that HIV infection must be considered yet another form of intimate partner violence; but, unlike physical abuse from which a woman usually recovers, without treatment HIV infection is ultimately fatal.

We should not placate ourselves with thinking that intimate partner violence and rape are confined to resource-poor countries. Data compiled from the U.S. is revealing. The U.S. Justice Department estimates that one in five U.S. women will experience rape or attempted rape during her college years, and that fewer than 5 percent of these rapes will be reported. Over the last two years, more than 787,000 women were the victims of rape or sexual assault. One in five American high school girls has been physically or sexually abused by a dating partner. Current research indicates that 25% of women in the U.S. have experience physical and/or sexual violence by a current or former partner. The Institute of Medicine estimated that 5 million women in the U.S. are physically, sexually, or emotionally abused by their sexual partners each year, and nearly 350,000 pregnant women are abused by their partners each year. Tragically, homicide is one of the leading causes of maternal deaths in the U.S. each year. The high rate of domestic violence in the U.S. has led some states to pass laws requiring mandatory reporting of domestic abuse when suspected by physicians and health care personnel. Despite all of the statistics, virtually no discussion of intimate partner violence occurs within the Christian church.

These numbers are sobering and certainly do not reflect the teachings of Jesus regarding respect for women. Given the extent of physical and sexual violence against women, the Church cannot remain silent—whether the violence occurs in countries distant from our own or within our own neighborhoods or Christian communities. When our Lord was confronted with an angry, vengeful crowd who dragged a woman accused of adultery before him, he protected her, spoke to her with respect, and sent her on her way with a challenge to "sin no more" (John 8:1–11). Jesus challenged the practice of easy divorce and urged monogamy, fidelity, and love. He welcomed Mary, Martha, and Mary Magdalene into his group of intimate followers. He urged that the homes of widows not be "devoured," as the teachers of the law were in the practice of doing (Mark 12:40). When Jesus accepted water at the well from the Samaritan woman, his own disciples "were surprised to find him talking with a woman" (John 4:27, NIV). Paul wrote to Timothy—and James also wrote—to remind the church to care especially for women who had lost their husbands and were vulnerable (1 Timothy 5:3; James 1:27).

What women experience in modern times is obviously not representative of what God intended and can be completely opposite of the way Jesus treated the women around him. In our era in fact, many young women are so deeply disrespected as to be drawn or pushed into the sex trade— tragically, sometimes by their own families. All over the world, women are being silenced, if not abused, and often prevented from gaining education and freedom under the pretext of religion. And in large parts of the world, women are at extreme risk of being infected with HIV because of the irresponsible and often violent sexual misbehavior of men. How does God view all of this? How does God view the silence and complicity of the rest of us, even if we are not personally a part of the rapacious mob? How are we to protect our sisters?

The Children

Who could be more vulnerable than a child? Children are a joy to their parents and families, and to all around them. But children can also be demanding, noisy, intrusive, expensive, and difficult in different ways. Their needs and wants are many and frequent. They can't do anything for themselves, at least in the earliest stages. They must be fed, or they will quickly weaken and die. They are prone to sickness, injury, and disease.

The extra layers of vulnerability upon some children may be consequences of cumulative effects of chronic circumstances or of a single catastrophic event: hunger/poverty, natural disasters, political or familial conflict, refugeeism, exploitive labor, or HIV infection.

If a woman infected with HIV becomes pregnant, her infant undergoes the risk of HIV infection as well. Without treatment, half of these infants will die by two years of age. Infants who do not become infected become orphans as they watch their parents' health gradually succumb to AIDS. As orphans lose the protection of their parents or relatives, they become the targets of nefarious members of society who seek them out for commercial gain. It is estimated that each year there are more than 2 million children, most of whom are orphans, drawn into the sex trade. These children may exchange sex for food to prevent starvation for themselves and their siblings. Repeated sexual encounters such as these may ultimately result in HIV infection, other sexually transmitted infections, and unwanted pregnancy. Additionally, a number of girls are taken by rebel militias, where the girls are frequently violated by members of the militia and by commanders, who take some of them as their "wives."

Indeed, hunger and poverty drive many children to absolutely desperate measures. Natural disasters may also increase the vulnerability of children. In 2006, the U.S. government responded to 54 disasters in 39 countries—affecting over 70 million children. Disasters often result in the loss of shelters and infrastructure necessary to maintain stable food supplies and income for families. Disability or the death of family members further increases the level of vulnerability that children experience.

Often etched in our minds are the pictures of children caught in the midst of conflict. In 2006, the U.S. government estimated that there were more than 20 million children worldwide who had lost access to shelter, food, and basic services as a result of conflict. Aside from the basic amenities that these children lose, children in communities involved in conflict are deprived of their spiritual and psychological well-being and are at risk for separation from their parents as well as other sources of psychological, social, economic, and spiritual support.

Child refugees are among the most vulnerable populations in the world. As of 2006, the United Nations High Commissioner for Refugees estimated that there were more than 21 million refugees, internally displaced individuals, returnees, asylum seekers, stateless persons, and others; 9 million of those were children.

And as if misfortunes such as hunger, poverty, conflict, and refugeeism are not enough for children who survive infancy, a cruel fate awaits some in the form of sweatshops and unhealthy, dangerous work. Statistics from 2004 from international aid organizations estimated that there were 218 million children aged 5 to 17 who were engaged in child labor, of whom 50% worked in hazardous conditions.

The impact of HIV on families even further increases the vulnerability of children, stripping away the psychosocial, spiritual, and economic support that is vital to children's well-being. Due to HIV, children can become alienated from their communities and schools, creating an entire generation of children with poor health, minimal marketable skills, inadequate levels of education, and nonexistent financial resources. HIV thus amplifies all of the negative factors that are associated with the perpetuation of poverty among populations that are already poor.

Two episodes reported in Matthew's Gospel display Jesus's attitude toward these matters. Both of these teach that children are to be viewed as treasures and not commodities for exploitation.

> Then people brought little children to Jesus for him to place his hands on them and pray for them. But the disciples rebuked them. Jesus said, "Let the little children come to me, and do not hinder them, for the kingdom of heaven belongs to such as these." When he had placed his hands on them, he went on from there. (Matthew 19:13–15)

> At that time the disciples came to Jesus and asked, "Who, then, is the greatest in the kingdom of heaven?" He called a little child to him, and placed the child among them. And he said: "Truly I tell you, unless you change and become like little children, you will never enter the kingdom of heaven. Therefore, whoever takes the lowly position of this child is the greatest in the kingdom of heaven. And whoever welcomes one such child in my name welcomes me. If anyone causes one of these little ones—those who believe in me—to stumble, it would be better for them to have a large millstone hung around their neck and to be drowned in the depths of the sea." (Matthew 18:1–6)

The fact that God himself would arrive in our world in the form of a vulnerable baby also says a great deal. Popular expectation would have the Messiah arrive like Superman, flying in and landing on Mt. Olympus. Instead he comes as a baby. And he warns that all of his followers, without exception, must become like little children if they would enter the kingdom of heaven. He warns in the strongest of language that, for anyone who mistreats a child who believes in him, it would be better to be thrown into the ocean strapped to a millstone. Ever countercultural, Jesus lays gentle hands on the children around him and blesses them.

Could anything be clearer? The children of the world—not just the children in my family, though that is where I must start—must be protected, welcomed, and blessed. Protecting them from HIV and other disease, from hunger and nakedness, from violence and cruelty, from danger and exploitation, from ignorance and disrespect—these objectives must be at the top of our list. This is not a cultural or regional issue, but a global issue in the eyes of the God of all peoples and nations.

The global impact of HIV on children is too frequently overlooked. While the emphasis is on the number of adults infected with HIV, there are 16 million orphans as a consequence of HIV infection of one or both parents, with 3 million new orphans added each year. This is a staggering number of children, overwhelming faith-based and other organizations that have historically cared for orphans. The creation of large orphanages—a traditional means of caring for orphans—is not only economically prohibitive but also contributes to the stigmatization of HIV orphans, concentrating them in buildings that are readily identified as, "That's where HIV orphans live." Orphaned children are better cared for in their communities, where they can interact with other children and receive the nurturing provided by family and community members. Providing support to family members to integrate orphaned children into a typical family structure—similar to foster care—has been found to be less expensive and emotionally, spiritually, and socially more effective. It is an opportunity for the Christian church to welcome children just as Jesus did. However, as with women infected with HIV, the Christian community has been slow to respond and, too often, has contributed to the stigmatization of HIV orphans by either ignoring their needs or refusing them a refuge through Christian ministries.

Tragically, orphans who are infected with HIV may be ignored, even by the largest and wealthiest Christian orphan organizations, because the cost of caring for an orphan infected with HIV is considered unaffordable. Additional drugs to treat HIV infection and the complications of HIV, along with more frequent physician and hospital visits, add $300 or more annually to the costs of orphan care. It is easier to ignore the problems associated with HIV infection entirely either by not finding out which orphans are infected, or, if infected, by not offering treatment. The outcome is the same. Without treatment, 50% of orphans who have HIV will die by 2 years of age. It is hard to imagine this situation within the Christian community when the teaching of Jesus is clear regarding our responsibilities to children, whom we are to emulate if we care to enter the kingdom of heaven.

The Elderly

At the opposite end of the age spectrum from children are the elderly. We all know how vulnerable the elderly are to disease, to stumbling and falling, and to losses of memory, vision, balance, and other faculties. Primarily age-related conditions like Alzheimer's and dementia can hit the elderly hard.

Our culture of youth tends to deprecate the elderly. A lifetime of faithful service to a company can be terminated in a moment if a younger, more productive, less expensive replacement is available for hire.

It may seem strange to talk about the elderly in the context of HIV, especially since the HIV epidemic is frequently characterized as occurring primarily in young, sexually active adults. But as parents with HIV lose the battle and their children become orphans, elderly grandparents—especially grandmothers—are called on to become the sole caregivers for their grandchildren. Having raised their own children only to see them die of HIV, these grandparents again become parents, but at a time when their health, strength, and endurance is waning.

The Christian community must recognize their responsibilities for coming alongside the elderly who now care for young children without mothers and fathers. They need the help of the Church to handle the responsibilities of feeding, nurturing, educating, and caring for their orphaned grandchildren. These children need the spiritual and emotional support of the Christian community for a hopeful future. Again, it is an opportunity to demonstrate the compassion that is demanded from those who believe in the teachings of the Old and New Testaments.

Jesus criticized the religious leaders of his time for failing to care for their parents and violating the fifth commandment on the pretext of making religious donations instead (Mark 7:9–13). Paul instructs Timothy, "Do not rebuke an older man harshly, but exhort him as if he were your father. Treat younger men as brothers, older women as mothers, and younger women as sisters, with absolute purity. Give proper recognition to those widows who are really in need. But if a widow has children or grandchildren, these should learn first of all to put their religion into practice by caring for their own family and so repaying their parents and grandparents, for this is pleasing to God" (1 Timothy 5:1–4). And just as God sanctifies infancy and childhood by the birth, infancy and childhood of Jesus, he sanctifies advanced age by the fulfillment of the promise of faith in century-old Abraham and Sarah! This is certainly not the way our culture would write the script.

It has often been observed that the commandment to "honor your father and mother" is not based on "because they have earned it," but rather on the promise of God's blessing. In our era, we must go against the trends and honor and protect our elders, especially as their vulnerabilities increase and they assume the unexpected load of having to act as parents for their grandchildren at a time when their own needs are increasing. HIV alters the family structure for the elderly: When their adult children die, older persons once again become head of the household. The problem is great. The number of grandparents caring for their orphaned grandchildren has doubled as a consequence of HIV. It is estimated that over half of the 16 million HIV orphans are cared for by their grandparents.

An understudied aspect of the HIV epidemic is the impact of the creation of hundreds of thousands of elderly caretakers. Grandparents are most often unprepared for returning to the responsibility of caring for children, either economically or physically. In caring first for their adult children with HIV and then also for their grandchildren, poverty and old age collide—creating circumstances of great need that neither they nor secular support systems are prepared, or sometimes even willing, to shoulder. Grandparents take on these commitments often willingly but also out of compulsion, realizing that, without their help, their adult children and their grandchildren may be abandoned. If their adult children have died from HIV, the grandparents become the sole caretakers of the orphaned children with little support from the community, the government, or other organizations.

In spite of the overwhelming responsibilities, elderly grandparents often remain hidden to aid organizations and perhaps to the Christian church as well. The fear of discrimination and stigmatization may contribute to grandparents' not asking for assistance, even it may be available. Additional obstacles include the generation gaps in knowledge about HIV and the difficulties the elderly might have in traveling to health care clinics, administering medicine with failing eyesight, and advocating for their orphaned grandchildren.

International organizations such as WHO have provided recommendations for assisting the elderly in caring for their adult children and grandchildren. These include providing financial support; training social and health service workers in the special needs of the elderly; and providing psychosocial support, medical support, and special training for elderly caregivers. Conspicuously absent from their recommendations is the provision of spiritual support or engaging the Christian Church in meeting the needs of the elderly who find themselves in circumstances that overwhelm almost every aspect of their daily lives.

The Christian community, responding to the clear instructions given in both the Old and New Testaments to care for the widows and orphans and to honor the elderly, has a unique opportunity to respond to a much-neglected aspect of the HIV epidemic.

The Poor

The case for God caring about the poor, the hungry, and those with inadequate clothing and shelter is overwhelming. The laws of ancient Israel insisted that *everyone* should have a Sabbath rest—not just the boss or the wealthy. In addition:

- "But during the seventh year let the land lie unplowed and unused. Then the poor among your people may get food from it, and the wild animals may eat what is left. Do the same with your vineyard and your olive grove." (Exodus 23:11)

- "Do not go over your vineyard a second time or pick up the grapes that have fallen. Leave them for the poor and the foreigner. I am the LORD your God." (Leviticus 19:10)

- "When you reap the harvest of your land, do not reap to the very edges of your field or gather the gleanings of your harvest. Leave them for the poor and for the foreigner residing among you. I am the LORD your God." (Leviticus 23:22)

- "However, there need be no poor people among you, for in the land the LORD your God is giving you to possess as your inheritance, he will richly bless you." (Deuteronomy 15:4)

Those who loudly claim that they want a "Christian country" might have more credibility if what they proposed had more of this biblical spirit and less self-serving market fundamentalism.

The Psalms, Proverbs, and Prophets make a strong and continual case for caring for the poor. Here is just a small sample of the biblical teaching:

- "'Because the poor are plundered and the needy groan, I will now arise,' says the LORD. 'I will protect them from those who malign them.'" (Psalm 12:5)

- "You evildoers frustrate the plans of the poor, but the LORD is their refuge." (Psalm 14:6)

- "I know that the LORD secures justice for the poor and upholds the cause of the needy." (Psalm 140:12)

- "He upholds the cause of the oppressed and gives food to the hungry. The LORD sets prisoners free." (Psalm 146:7)

- "An unplowed field produces food for the poor, but injustice sweeps it away." (Proverbs 13:23)

- "It is a sin to despise one's neighbor, but blessed is the one who is kind to the needy." (Proverbs 14:21)

- "Whoever oppresses the poor shows contempt for their Maker, but whoever is kind to the needy honors God." (Proverbs 14:31)

- "Whoever is kind to the poor lends to the LORD, and he will reward them for what they have done." (Proverbs 19:17)

- "And if you spend yourselves in behalf of the hungry and satisfy the needs of the oppressed, then your light will rise in the darkness, and your night will become like the noonday." (Isaiah 58:10)

- "The Spirit of the Sovereign LORD is on me, because the LORD has anointed me to proclaim good news to the poor. He has sent me to bind up the brokenhearted, to proclaim freedom for the captives and release from darkness for the prisoners." (Isaiah 61:1)

Of course, Jesus and the early Church make the same case in similar language:

- "Sell your possessions and give to the poor. Provide purses for your-selves that will not wear out, a treasure in heaven that will never fail, where no thief comes near and no moth destroys." (Luke 12:33)

- "But when you give a banquet, invite the poor, the crippled, the lame, the blind." (Luke 14:13)

- "If your enemy is hungry, feed him; if he is thirsty, give him something to drink. In doing this, you will heap burning coals on his head." (Romans 12:20)

- "Suppose a man comes into your meeting wearing a gold ring and fine clothes, and a poor man in filthy old clothes also comes in. If you show special attention to the man wearing fine clothes and say, 'Here's a good seat for you,' but say to the poor man, 'You stand there' or 'Sit on the floor by my feet,' have you not discriminated among yourselves and becomes judges with evil thoughts? Listen, my dear brothers and sisters: Has not God chosen those who are poor in the eyes of the world to be rich in faith and to inherit the kingdom he promised those who love him? But you have dishonored the poor. Is it not the rich who are exploiting you? Are they not the ones who are dragging you into court?" (James 2:2–6)

- "If anyone has material possessions and sees a brother or sister in need but has no pity on them, how can the love of God be in that person? Dear children, let us not love with words or speech but with actions and in truth." (1 John 3:17–18)

So often, those who suffer and who are vulnerable as children or as women are also poor. While the association between poverty and HIV is not entirely clear, it is quite certain that HIV pushes families and individuals into poverty. Poverty, in turn, reinforces people's captivity to their vulnerable circumstances. It is not surprising that there is a strong link between poverty and the HIV epidemic, especially as it affects women.

Often the poorest households are headed by women, who, if they are HIV-infected, bear the burden of caring for their own health as well as that of their children, whether the children have HIV or not. When poverty and HIV infection converge, women are most likely to be overwhelmed by the spiritual, emotional, psychosocial, nutritional, and educational needs of their families. Without adequate economic and educational resources for their children, a new generation struggling with poverty is likely.

The aggregate factors associated with poverty are frequently termed "culture of poverty," with the recognition that children of those who are poor often become poor in subsequent generations. Poverty is associated with low levels of education and literacy, and few skills that can be used to generate income. Thus, health and health care for people who are poor remains substandard and result in low labor productivity, further contributing to poverty. By definition, poor households generally have few financial assets, and thus they are often politically and socially marginalized. Such social exclusion makes it harder for families to garner appropriate economic and health resources. Women who find themselves as heads of households and mired in severe poverty may engage in commercial sexual transactions for economic gain but then find themselves infected with sexually transmitted diseases such as HIV, which further contributes to their isolation, stigmatization, and reduced ability to provide family support.

The poverty associated with HIV infection produces economic circumstances similar to those of any chronic illness by preventing individuals from living productive lives. Unlike many other chronic illnesses, however, HIV infection may affect multiple members in the same family, including the husband, the wife, and the children. Unlike other illnesses that may have a short duration, HIV is a chronic disease that affects an individual for an extended amount of time—in a situation where little or no medical help is available, often an eight- to ten-year period during which the person who is ill requires constant attention and support. Women and children who have HIV may be viewed as an additional economic burden to other family members and may be dismissed or subject to severe forms of discrimination. The local Christian church may also view these women and children as not contributing to the welfare of the church or as requiring substantial or even burdensome support from members of the Christian community.

Poverty also reduces the capacity of women to deal with the effects of HIV. For example, the likelihood of HIV transmission from a mother with HIV to her infant can be decreased if the mother formula-feeds rather than breast-feeds her baby, as breast milk contains significant amounts of HIV that can infect the infant as long as breast-feeding is continued. Under circumstances of poverty, the cost of formula is prohibitive. Although there are now potent drugs to treat HIV, the cost of the drugs, limited local availability of these drugs and transportation costs to health centers to obtain the drugs and care, usually prevents access to lifesaving treatment. Poverty even extends to an inability to pay for funeral and burial costs.

A child's chance of escaping from poverty is dependent on resources that are absent because of poverty. These resources—usually nonexistent or inconsistent—include education, marketable skills, socialization, access to financial resources, and loss-of-property rights. Large numbers of children who are trapped in poverty may adopt the very behaviors that contribute to poverty in the first place—young girls in particular engage in sex for money for economic survival, only to eventually succumb to HIV infection. The premature death of parents from HIV encourages children to marry earlier, drop out of school to support the family, and engage in hazardous work. When both parents die, the oldest child often becomes the head of the household, assuming full responsibility for the younger siblings.

The Sick

A sickness or injury can lead to various kinds of rejection by others. Worry about "catching" the infection, embarrassment and awkwardness, impatience—all of these reactions can leave the sick in a more vulnerable position than ever, precisely when they are most in need of help.

For Jesus, healing was central:

- "Jesus went throughout Galilee, teaching in their synagogues, proclaiming the good news of the kingdom, and healing every disease and sickness among the people." (Matthew 4:23)

- "When evening came, many who were demon-possessed were brought to him, and he drove out the spirits with a word and healed all the sick. This was to fulfill what was spoken through the prophet Isaiah: 'He took up our infirmities and bore our diseases.'" (Matthew 8:16–17)

- "And wherever he went—into villages, towns or countryside—they placed the sick in the marketplaces. They begged him to let them touch even the edge of his cloak, and all who touched it were healed." (Mark 6:56)

Jesus commissioned first his twelve disciples (Luke 9:2) and then the seventy (Luke 10:9) to do the same kind of healing. The early apostolic church carried on the same ministry: "Is anyone among you sick? Let them call the elders of the church to pray over them and anoint them with oil in the name of the Lord. And the prayer offered in faith will make the sick person well; the Lord will raise them up" (James 5:14–15a).

It is well known how HIV has frightened many people away from its victims, much as leprosy did in times past. But the church of Jesus Christ must never leave the sick unattended, uncared for, and vulnerable. Healing the sick is at the very heart of our life and calling. Caring for women and children with HIV must be viewed by the Christian community as an opportunity to live out the teachings of Jesus.

The Stranger

Finally, we must note how the stranger is vulnerable. The stranger can seem mysterious and threatening at times—but the reality is that it is the stranger who is outnumbered and more vulnerable. The stranger could be someone of another race or nationality, someone who looks different or speaks a different language, or someone who practices a different religion. The ignorant among us will be tempted to play on their personal (and our own) fears and perhaps stereotype, stigmatize, or even attack the stranger. HIV contributes to individuals' becoming strangers in their own households, friendships, families, and communities through stigmatization and isolation. Women who are HIV-infected become separated from spiritual, social, and family support mechanisms, forcing them to withdraw and internalize their concerns—thereby reducing their access to desperately needed support mechanisms. Even the support systems that are available are often inundated with the work of helping others with chronic diseases—often those with less stigma.

We must persist. God's promise to Abraham (Genesis 12:3) was that in Abraham and his descendants "all peoples on earth" would be blessed. Throughout the Old and New Testaments, the stranger and alien are drawn into the people of God. In the accounts of Rahab, Melchizedek, Ruth, the Good Samaritan, the Wise Men (Magi) from the East, Cornelius—and even in the breaking down of the wall between Jews and Gentiles (Ephesians 2), and in the promise that in the New Jerusalem all the nations will be represented and all will bring their contributions into the city (Revelation 5:9—21:24–26)—there is a consistent, robust challenge to embrace the stranger, to show hospitality and care.

It is hard enough to care for those who are sick, for vulnerable women and children, for those who are poor among our own kind! But the problems transcend the capacity of each group to take care of its own. We need a collaborative effort among nations and organizations, including the Christian community, that cuts across our typical divisions and identities. Biblical faith challenges us to risk our own insecurities and fears and to reach out to the vulnerable stranger.

Two Basic Reasons to Respond

As we look over this perhaps daunting list of those who are vulnerable and see the need for a response, two reasons are immediately clear: compassion and justice. Compassion literally means "to suffer with," to come alongside someone because we feel the pain they experience. We empathize and sympathize with the hurting. We identify in some way with their vulnerability and are moved to want to stand alongside and help, encourage, and comfort. Do we have a tender heart? Is the spiritual fruit of kindness and mercy manifest in our hearts and minds? We have received mercy, but will we show it to others?

But it is not just compassion that drives our response; it is also justice. The vulnerable have a kind of "right" to our help. The world in general thinks that "rights" are just political fiction: Governmental bodies decide what constitutional rights to grant their citizens; but what they give, they could take away. Biblical people think of rights and duties as something based in God's will and judgment. It is God who grants human rights to people. Every man, woman, and child on the face of the earth has been created in God's image and likeness, and is the object of his redeeming love on the cross. This is why, ultimately, all people have a right to our care and to fairness and justice from us. So yes, we are being kind and generous when we reach out to help others; but we must always remember the other side: It is not just about kindness and compassion. These people *deserve* to be helped and treated with care and respect because they are God's own, beloved creatures.

To put it another way, we are showing our love for God and for our neighbor when we care for the vulnerable and needy. It is an act of love. But it is also an act of obedience. God commands and guides us to care for our neighbor and for the poor and needy. This is not an optional part of our faith—not a voluntary act of love and generosity alone—but an essential duty, an obligation growing from our faith and covenant with Jesus as our Lord and leader.

Valuing Vulnerability

One perspective not to be overlooked is the value of vulnerability as a means. Vulnerability is not an "end"—not the goal of life—but it is a "means" to the end. Let's look again at the passage in 1 Corinthians (1:26–29): "Brothers and sisters, think of what you were when you were called. Not many of you were wise by human standards; not many were influential; not many were of noble birth. But God chose the foolish things of the world to shame the wise; God chose the weak things of the world to shame the strong. God chose the lowly things of this world and the despised things—and the things that are not—to nullify the things that are, so that no one may boast before him." In his second letter to the Corinthians, Paul famously wrote:

"But we have this treasure in jars of clay to show that this all-surpassing power is from God and not from us" (2 Corinthians 4:7).

Our weakness and emptiness makes room for the reality of God to shine through. By reaching out in care and love to the vulnerable and hurting, we may experience what the Letter to the Hebrews describes (13:2): "Do not forget to show hospitality to strangers, for by so doing some people have shown hospitality to angels without knowing it." God has room to show up in the lives of the weak. God's wisdom is sometimes more easily displayed among people who, by worldly standards, are not so full of their own human intelligence and learning. God's smile sometimes can be more visible on the faces of those without the standard definitions of a beautiful or handsome appearance. God's creativity may have more room to emerge among those who are not the elite entrepreneurs in our midst.

By reaching out and investing our time and care among the vulnerable and weak, we may see truly extraordinary evidence of God at work. And not only will we leave with a greater blessing than we brought; we will be learning that lesson for our own lives: I must decrease so God can increase. I must be poor in spirit to make room for the kingdom of heaven to bless my life.

Conclusion: We Are All Poor; We Are All Redeemers

We who are so blessed—we who are by the world's standards, "rich"—have such an obligation and such an opportunity to serve our Lord and our neighbors. But it is crucial to remember the rebuke to the church at Laodicea in the book of Revelation (3:17–20): "You say, 'I am rich; I have acquired wealth and do not need a thing.' But you do not realize that you are wretched, pitiful, poor, blind and naked. I counsel you to buy from me gold refined in the fire, so you can become rich; and white clothes to wear, so you can cover your shameful nakedness; and salve to put on your eyes, so you can see. Those whom I love I rebuke and discipline. So be earnest and repent. Here I am! I stand at the door and knock. If anyone hears my voice and opens the door, I will come in and eat with that person, and they with me."

The reality is that we are no better, no richer, no stronger than anyone else. We, too, are vulnerable in our own ways, and we, too, need help from others. Those whom we come alongside to help, we will find helping us in our own poverty and vulnerability. We come to wash the feet of others, but our own feet get washed as well. We teach, but we also listen and watch and learn. We give, but we also receive.

Genesis 1 teaches us that we are made in the image and likeness of God, our Creator. But our Creator is also our Redeemer. We must understand that we are made in the image and likeness of the Redeemer. So it is embedded in our human nature, our DNA, that we need to express creativity in our lives to be fully human. And so we must also find scope and opportunity to act redemptively to be fully human. God is love; we are made in the image of the God who is love. If we try to quench or stifle our love for others, including the vulnerable and those in need of our redemptive help, we dehumanize ourselves.

In the end, our biblical theology teaches us that we reach out to help the vulnerable (1) because they need it and deserve it, (2) because God commands and invites us to do so, and, finally, (3) because it is essential to our own life if we want to experience it to the full.

Additional Reading

Gill, David. *Becoming Good: Building Moral Character.* Downers Grove IL: InterVarsity, 2000.

———. *Doing Right: Practicing Ethical Principles.* Downers Grove, IL: InterVarsity, 2004.

Joslin, Daphne. *Invisible Caregivers: Older Adults Raising Children in the Wake of HIV/AIDS.* New York: Columbia University Press, 2002.

Williams, Alun. *Ageing and Poverty in Africa: Ugandan Livelihoods in a Time of HIV/AIDS.* Burlington, VT: Ashgate, 2003.

8

A Christian Look at Suffering in a Time of HIV

SUSAN S. PHILLIPS

And I heard a loud voice from the throne saying, "Now the dwelling of God is with people, and he will live with them. They will be his people, and God himself will be with them and be their God. He will wipe every tear from their eyes. There will be no more death or mourning or crying or pain, for the old order of things has passed away." (Revelation 21:3–4)

Yearning toward the New Order

GOD'S DWELLING PLACE IS among people, and God is making all things new. Death, grief, mourning, and pain will come to an end. This is the promise people of faith yearn toward in the midst of interminable suffering and what so often seems like intermittent grace. We trust that God is with us, and we also know that, until that new order is fully in place, there will be grievous suffering that staggers, baffles, stigmatizes, and wounds. We are asked to look toward the future with hope. And the command to look also directs us to the reality of the people among whom God dwells. As we look, we see suffering of varying magnitudes and forms. In particular, the enormous suffering throughout the world due to the HIV epidemic—much of it borne by women—grips our attention. Prodigious work has been done to stem the tide of that suffering as well as to tend those afflicted by it, yet the tide of suffering keeps rising.

Recently I spoke with "Martha," an African woman from a large Sub-Saharan country. She has been infected with HIV for nearly twenty years. She has been receiving treatment for more than ten years and now radiates health and hope, even as she speaks about her suffering. When she was first infected, and for many years afterwards, she didn't know it. Her husband died in the mid 1990s after years of illnesses and a final coma lasting three months. Eight months later, while she was still wearing the black of mourning, her precious three-year-old daughter died. She was told the cause was cerebral malaria. Family members declared there was a curse on those who had died, and they responded to her grief in hurtful ways. Martha says that about 1 percent of her wondered if her loved ones died from the disease about which no one spoke.

Reeling from loss and the unkindness of family members, Martha and her remaining child, an eight-year-old son, came for a visit to a friend in California. Shortly after arriving, her son fell ill and comatose. The caregivers at the hospital asked Martha for permission to test him for HIV. Martha said, "All I knew about HIV was that it was a death sentence. I told them I needed time to decide about the test." After a day, she decided to have him tested. When she learned he was infected with the virus, he was already doing better, thanks to the medications he was receiving. Martha was also tested and told she was infected.

In Martha's home country, people infected with HIV were shunned and stigmatized. They weren't allowed to shake hands with others, share food, be together in classrooms, or sleep in the same room. Some children with the illness were abandoned. Going back home was not an option. However, her friend in California had the same rejecting reaction, so Martha and her son found themselves at the mercy of strangers. Those strangers, all in the field of caring for people with HIV, were kind and loving. They helped Martha create a stable life for herself and her son as they began receiving treatments. In the years since diagnosis, Martha herself has become an advocate for people who are HIV-infected, establishing an aid organization, traveling back to her country, and helping women face their illness and receive healing treatment.

Bearing Witness to Affliction

Martha works mostly with widows. Many of these women's husbands have died in the epidemic of HIV, often without knowing the cause. The widows suffer bereavement, social marginalization, often poverty (that, for some, leads to prostitution), and, far too often, infection as well. Martha listens to the suffering of the women and broaches the subject of getting tested for HIV. Now, with new treatments available, she's able to counter the belief that testing positive would be a death sentence. She says, "This is not the end of the world . . . Look at me. I can come with you for testing, and you can get medications like I have." Some tell her that they think their husbands died of another illness, possibly from a lethal curse. Remembering her own experience, Martha asks, "Doesn't maybe 1 percent of you wonder if it might be the virus?" Many have admitted that, yes, there is that possibility.

With Martha's caring support and encouragement, women have been tested and have received lifesaving treatment. An African man who is HIV-positive who is doing work similar to Martha's wrote, "I have given hope, I hope, to some people" (see "Winstone Zulu" in Nolan, 222). These advocates for hope and healing have had the courage to face their own illness and now come alongside others to help them do the same.

The act of looking at suffering is significant. It's painful to bear witness to suffering, especially when the suffering is extreme and widespread, and our ability to ameliorate it is so small. Witnessing suffering can visit suffering on the observer, and so doing it takes courage. Martha feels God has given her this work and strengthened her for it. A widow in Africa calls her "an angel," and Martha laughs as she recounts that, speaking of her happiness in saving a few lives. She says, "God gave me courage. God wanted to save my life and for me to save others."

We can lack courage in the face of suffering. Having mustered the wherewithal to witness suffering, we find too often that the combined experience of shock, fear, and impotence evoke from us an unholy, yet wholly human reaction that ends up adding insult to injury. When this happens, we participate in suffering. People exhort the homeless, banish the leper, mock the loser, and shame the disabled and different among us. Those affected by the HIV epidemic have experienced such reactions. Jesus, too, received this treatment, and looking at his life forever reminds us of our tendencies toward such responses.

To Fail to Attend to Suffering Is to Compound It

Our faith calls us to look, bear witness, pay attention. Part of what we attend to is suffering in all its complexity. To fail to attend to suffering is to compound it. Writing in the throes of the twentieth-century European Holocaust, Simone Weil identified complex suffering as "affliction." She wrote, "There is not real affliction unless the event which has gripped and uprooted a life attacks it, directly or indirectly, in all its parts, social, psychological, and physical" (see "The Love of God and Affliction," in Panichas, 440–41).

The epidemic of HIV in Africa is one of affliction. It grips and uproots lives. For a variety of reasons, it targets those who are already among the socially marginalized: women and their children. Drawing attention to the situation of women in twenty-first-century Africa, the Democratic Republic of Congo section of the Circle of African Women Theologians stated that "the woman is the victim of violence from all sides and in her many roles: first in her family as a child; next as a young woman; then in her marriage as wife and mother; finally, in her social environment as a worker or colleague. She suffers violence . . ." (Beya, 185). These African women theologians claim that, at all stages of life, many African women today are suffering the multifaceted, life-uprooting affliction of gender-related violence. Into this already-existing suffering has come the pandemic of HIV, with women now constituting more than 60 percent of all HIV infections in Sub-Saharan Africa, an area containing approximately 70 percent of the more than 23 million global infections (see Hunter, 6, and global statistics from http://data.unaids.org/pub/Report/2009/JC1700_Epi_Update_2009_en.pdf). These are some facets of suffering to which we bear witness even while we trust that God is dwelling with us.

Love, Meaning, and the Questions Suffering Elicits

We are all acquainted with suffering. All people will experience and undergo pain and, eventually, die. Suffering may afflict us in many dimensions of our lives. Even when suffering is expected, chosen, or allowed, we come under its thrall and are changed by it. We emerge from what we have undergone, altered in some respect. We may be freed from pain, as can be the case with surgery, or rendered subject to ongoing agony, as with dismemberment. We may be strengthened by suffering, as steel is tempered by fire, or debilitated, mutilated, and scarred. As storied beings, we seek meaning from suffering. Even the suffering that is most vehemently protested and rejected becomes part of our narrative and part of the tales told by our people.

Religious people tell stories of suffering. From Latin (*religare*), the word *religion* has to do with binding together. Religion involves binding that takes the form of relying on God, and it binds people to one another with the ligaments of love and justice. Religion also offers the bonds of meaning, providing hermeneutical bridges across which our minds travel when trying to make sense of our lives and our world. We suffer in the context of our connections to God and others, and we understand our suffering in relation to our religious beliefs. Christian Scripture tells us that when we do right and suffer, we are in God's grace and in solidarity with Jesus who suffered (see, for example, 1 Peter 2:20–21).

The Judeo-Christian religion affirms a God who suffers for people. The Hebrew prophets and the Gospel tell us about the suffering servant who was despised and rejected, yet came with the message of mercy for all. Made in that God's image, we suffer, though suffering often seems inexplicable—even wrong. Suffering elicits desires for relief, justice, support, and consolation. Like the one we follow, we suffer and we serve. And, in keeping with that *imago Christi*, we ask questions. We do so especially in situations of extreme affliction, like the one scorching people afflicted by HIV.

In our quest for understanding, questions of cross-cultural significance may be helpful. Contrarily, questioning can also be a strategy wielded out of fear and can itself serve to exacerbate suffering. Over the course of many years of teaching counselors, chaplains, spiritual directors, and ministers about attending to those who are suffering, I've found it helpful to think in terms of the questions—helpful and unhelpful—that arise from the experience of suffering.

What?

We ask, "What?" Some forms of this question seek diagnosis in the hope of treatment. They have spurred research and the development of preventive strategies and lifesaving remedies. We also ask, "What is the nature of the suffering?" This is an orienting question that seeks meaning and helps us enter the experience of the one suffering, even when that one is the self. Possible answers to this question are manifold, their ranges including:

- mild—extreme
- brief—chronic
- shared—isolating
- focused—pervasive
- chosen—not chosen
- self-inflicted—imposed—befallen
- comprehensible—bewildering
- manageable—enslaving
- remembered—present—anticipated
- intended—accidental
- accepted—protested
- peripheral—central
- ennobling—shaming
- corrective—warping
- redemptive—condemning
- constructive—destructive

Illness and pain are colored by meaning-laden experience, and we listen and watch in order to catch hue and tone. Increasingly, stories from the epidemic—like Martha's—are helping us learn about the experience of those afflicted with HIV. In the 2004 South African film *Yesterday* (written and directed by Darrell Roodt), about a fictional Zulu husband and wife both afflicted with HIV, we see the full import of the illness dawn on them and take over their lives. The wife is the first to be diagnosed. She had been experiencing a cough, at first mild and focused, but increasingly strong and central to her life. The diagnosis tells her that the physical suffering's origin is itself a source of suffering, coming as it does through her beloved husband's infidelity. The origin magnifies the suffering as does the suffering's prognosis: Infected in a time and place with no effective treatment for the disease, both she and her husband will die, leaving behind their young daughter. Holding this knowledge privately, she travels to the city to tell her migrant laborer husband about what has befallen them. Driven out of his mind by the horrendous news and all it communicates, he beats her. Her suffering compounds.

Before long, the husband, debilitated and deformed by the disease, returns to his wife in the village and depends on her care as he dies. The village people reject them, fearing the illness and blaming the ill. Simone Weil identified the three elements of affliction as physical pain, distress of soul, and social degradation. The woman named Yesterday was afflicted, and part of her affliction was cultural, for women in her culture bear a disproportionate burden in the HIV epidemic.

Even so, Yesterday is powerfully motivated by love and acts effectively to shape her life and the lives of her husband and daughter (whose HIV status the film viewer does not learn). What matters and what is possible become clear to the wife as the film progresses. On the outskirts of town, she constructs a small building for her husband to lie in as he dies. She labors alone, except for the assistance of her preschool-aged daughter. She cares for her husband and then buries him. She vows to live until her daughter begins school, and she does so. Throughout her suffering, she serves others in love.

Yesterday has one friend, a schoolteacher, and that friend is a source of grace. Through her eyes we see the nobility of the wife, and through her voice we hear protest against the fearful judgments of the neighbors. The teacher offers practical help in the present and for the future, telling the dying woman that once she is gone, she will love and care for the orphaned daughter as her own. She bears witness to the "what"s of Yesterday's suffering, and she acts to alleviate them.

Why?

In the face of suffering, especially extreme suffering like that borne by all women afflicted by HIV, we also ask, "Why?" Sometimes we turn the questions to God as Job did, trusting God to answer him. Jesus, too, dying on the cross asked, "Why?" However, in Scripture neither God nor Jesus offer direct answers to sufferers' "why" questions.

Many answers to the question "Why?" presume to judge God or the suffering person. We ask, "Why do good people suffer when God is all-powerful and all-loving?" (or Rabbi Harold Kushner's version, "Why do bad things happen to good people?"). The tension lies in seeing God as all-powerful, all-knowing, all-good, and, therefore, capable of preventing unjust and/or extreme suffering. There are those who resolve the tension by viewing God as not all-good. Some who believe in God doubt divine omniscience, while others adjust the equation by reducing God's presumed power. For those who retain belief in the undiminished capacities of a God involved in human life, the "why" questions may be turned toward people. This enterprise of explaining and assigning responsibility for suffering has been called *theodicy*, and its various manifestations are alive and well today.

We who live in the twenty-first century, especially those in the global north, have witnessed humankind's increasing capacities for understanding the world; creating rational systems of government, commerce, and social life; and harnessing nature for our presumed well-being. We often see disease, disaster, and death as aberrations in a world that is largely subject to our control. Conversely, we see success, health, and longevity as personal achievements. So, when faced with inexplicable suffering, we ask "why" and often generate explanations that offer no voice, help, or consolation to those bearing the suffering.

Four Traditional Theodicies

There are four traditional forms of theodicy, theological explanations of why people suffer seemingly unjustly, sometimes extremely. Each of these ways of understanding suffering exists in Christian circles today.

Sin and Punishment

There is the view that we suffer because we sin and God punishes us. Especially in cases of unjust and extreme suffering, this view attributes cruelty to God. In situations of suffering resulting from natural disasters, human genocide, and torturous illness, we struggle to see how guilt precipitated these events. This, however, is the stance of ancient proverbial wisdom: Through moral living we can avoid suffering, and when we behave immorally, God punishes us. This view lingers despite our knowledge of Jesus's teachings, stories, and life. In speaking of a pastor who from the pulpit condemned HIV patients for their immoral lifestyles, Martha said, "Can't he think that there are some people here who are victims?"

Such condemnation is displayed in the film *Yesterday*, and it is such contempt and discrimination that has kept infected people around the world from speaking out about their suffering. An independent church leader in Botswana—expressing the view of many Christians in all parts of the world—said that HIV was "a punishment sent by God . . . Today we have all kinds of unnatural things . . . Christ is the one who said that those who do such things are cursed already" (quoted by Iliffe, 94).

Attempts to include all suffering in a paradigm of guilt and punishment offers, in Emmanuel Kant's words, "an apology in which the defense is worse than the charge . . . and may certainly be left to the detestation of everyone who has the least spark of morality" (*An Inquiry Critical and Metaphysical, Into the Grounds for Proof for the Existence of God and into Theodicy*, London, 1819, cited in Farley, 21). This is a stance of contempt: We blame the victim. Fear and the self-protective illusion that we can fully control our health and well-being lie beneath this cruel theodicy.

A Larger Aesthetic Harmony

This is the view that evil and suffering do not significantly undermine the goodness of creation; in fact, the suffering of some may allow for greater good from an ultimate perspective. The aesthetic harmony theodicy asserts that suffering is part of the created order, serving, perhaps, to illuminate the good and beautiful.

We see this view in secular thinking, too. Without attributing responsibility for suffering, we can see how suffering sometimes illuminates joy. V. S. Naipaul wrote: "Suffering is as elemental as night [and] . . . makes more keen the appreciation of happiness" (in a letter from Oxford to his older sister Kamla, quoted by Daphne Merkin in "Suffering, Elemental as Night," *New York Times Book Review*, 1 September 2002, 11). This view in its theological form, however, posits an indifferent God who plays dice with the universe for aesthetic pleasure. In the context of lives uprooted by disease and continents ravished by epidemic, it seems especially heretical to conceive of God as indifferent.

Throughout her tragic losses and journey toward healing, Martha has been a praying woman. She's talked to God, and when it looked as though she was going to lose her son in addition to her husband and daughter, she told God that if her son died, she would kill herself and he couldn't blame her for it. She did not say she asked God "Why?" She stayed in conversation with God. Clearly, she rejects a view of God as indifferent. She believes God, however inscrutable, is aware of the particulars of her life, spared her life and that of her son, and has given her lifesaving work to do. This is faith in the God who knows and loves us, not in a detached, game-playing deity.

Education

Some argue that God inflicts suffering for our refining, maturing, and strengthening. People speak to those in the grip of suffering about how God is teaching them through the experience. For example, we hear religious leaders claim that God has allowed a city to suffer a natural disaster because the city was sinful and needed to be taught a lesson.

The usefulness of the education explanation for suffering comes from the point of view of the one suffering. We can find sometimes, by God's grace, that good does come through suffering. Aeschylus, the Greek tragedian wrote: "He who learns must suffer" (*Agamemnon* l.177 [fourth century BCE]). Contemporary psychology essentially affirms that point of view, seeing change as prompted by pain or suffering. However, God is greatly diminished when viewed as an all-powerful schoolmaster rapping our knuckles with a ruler. We see the opposite in Jesus's parable of the Good Samaritan.

> "A man was going down from Jerusalem to Jericho, when he was attacked by robbers. They stripped him of his clothes, beat him and went away, leaving him half dead. A priest happened to be going down the same road, and when he saw the man, he passed by on the other side. So too, a Levite, when he came to the place and saw him, passed by on the other side. But a Samaritan, as he traveled, came where the man was; and when he saw him, he took pity on him. He went to him and bandaged his wounds, pouring on oil and wine. Then he put the man on his own donkey, brought him to an inn and took care of him. The next day he took out two denarii and gave them to the innkeeper. 'Look after him,' he said, 'and when I return, I will reimburse you for any extra expense you may have.' Which of these three do you think was a neighbor to the man who fell into the hands of robbers?" The expert in the law replied, "The one who had mercy on him." Jesus told him, "Go and do likewise." (Luke 10:30–37)

In a time of great suffering in my own life, a few loving Christians said to me, "God is making you stronger by giving you this suffering. It is a gift. Think how wise you will be made by it." I remember those words now, nearly thirty years later, and not because they were helpful or consoling. I do not believe God is just a schoolmaster, nor do I believe we are to invite suffering in order to learn from it. Day by day, more of Africa's inhabitants are either infected or affected by HIV. Everyone is bereft. Some African

Christians say, "We have AIDS" (see, for example, Mageto). This is a stance of solidarity in suffering, not one of masochistic, self-promoting piety.

Eschatological Hope

This theodicy has given comfort to those who find no hope in history, and no evidence on earth that evil and suffering are not the last words. The hope is that, though life has been a vale of tears, the one who dies moves on to a better place. This is, at best, a consolation, not a justification for suffering. However, in the most condemning responses to the HIV crisis, people have sometimes claimed the afflicted are deprived of this hope. One Adventist man at the funeral of his sister in Lusaka (Zambia) in 1991 announced to those present: "What worries me most is that she has missed heaven." In Kenya it was reported that people did not bury those who died of HIV because those people were "assumed not to have the chance of life-after-death" (Iliffe, 114).

Without denying the truth of this hope for the future as described in Scripture, that hope must not allow us to be apathetic, passive, and indifferent in the face of suffering and injustice. We live, struggle, think, act, and suffer on earth and in history, and we're called to behold that reality, as we also behold the promised future. Christian hope doesn't silence truth.

How?

The Christian theologian Dorothy Soelle poses two "how" questions about suffering that are crucial for us as Christians (Soelle, 5). The first is, "What are the causes of suffering, and how can these conditions be eliminated?"

This question is essential because those of us who ignore it will participate in the maintenance of the conditions responsible for the varieties of suffering that befall the majority of people. The danger of not assuming responsibility for the abolition of certain forms of suffering is the danger of becoming sadistic—of counseling endurance to the sufferers without a protest against the injustice of their suffering.

Martha, after receiving treatments for her infection, immediately took up the work of eliminating the conditions causing suffering in her home country. She raised money and dedicated her efforts to help people protect themselves from the virus and preserve their health when they were infected. Jesus calls us to participate in the work of health preservation.

The social, psychological, and spiritual suffering, which go beyond the sheer physical effects of the illness, can be ameliorated, too. The stigma of the illness isolates and disenfranchises the afflicted. Widows and orphans—subjects of discrimination for millennia—were of particular interest to Jesus, and their care has been part of the work of his Church. So, too, it should be today in the face of this epidemic. Sadly, many faithful churchgoers around the world who are infected with HIV don't disclose their status in church because they have been shunned or vilified when they've done so.

Soelle's second question is, "What is the meaning of suffering, and under what conditions [how] can it make us more human?" This question is essential because, as discussed previously, we make meaning out of our suffering. Though the suffering be due to impersonal forces and due to no fault of their own, nevertheless, people make meaning from it. This is not just a question for people afflicted with extreme suffering; it applies to all of us. How do we understand our lives in light of the suffering that marks them? What enables us to grow in goodness even as we suffer? Martha's suffering enabled her to embrace what she sees as her life's work, helping others infected with HIV. She would not choose the suffering, but she has found light shining in the darkness.

Those with illnesses and disabilities can remind us of our humanity. They are our teachers, for they face limitations like those that will, in all likelihood, affect each of us one day. God is always reaching toward people in love and, in Jesus Christ, expressed ultimate solidarity in taking on the suffering of mortality and death. This identification erases us–them divisions that can cause us to barricade our hearts, laugh, point our fingers, shake our heads, and pass by on the other side of the road.

Coming alongside people in their suffering helps both us and them to become more human and to find a way forward. For Martha, it was the people at the hospital in California that stood by her through her days of discovering that she and her son were infected. They remained with her, helping her find ways to live and heal in a foreign country. For Yesterday, it was the teacher friend in the village. That friend accompanied her from her first symptoms of illness through her husband's death and, eventually, her own. None of these companions to Martha and Yesterday were family members. None were church communities. This is a loss to the sick women, but also to the families and churches who could have participated in their care and been blessed in doing so.

Who?

It's real people who suffer, not statistical entities that can be registered and filed away. Winstone Zulu of Zambia wrote of his experience of being discriminated against because he has HIV. He's been pushed off buses, denied student visas, and told to avoid meat, alcohol, and sex. The discrimination has included "[h]aving special laws made for me. Being denied employment, promotion, insurance, God's blessing when marrying. Written off" (Nolan, 223). Many with HIV feel written off. Yet we affirm a God who calls us each by name, knows the hairs on our heads, and tells us that when we care for those who suffer, we participate in grace.

Suffering may be engulfing and afflicting, but when we truly encounter the person who is suffering, our hearts will be changed. We learn much from our African brothers and sisters—like Winstone Zulu and Martha—who have followed Jesus's example as they've cared for those with HIV. Jesus is our ultimate exemplar as we suffer and as we come alongside people in their suffering. We are taught by people, living today in all parts of the world, who have allowed God's grace to minister to them in their pain, just as we learn from those we read about in Scripture who received Jesus's care.

Jesus worked prophetically, taking a stance against injustice, and he attended to the person experiencing the suffering. Sometimes people asked for his help. Bartimaeus asked, and Jesus affirmed his faith (Mark 10:46–52). The Syrophoenician woman asked for healing for her daughter and begged, kneeling at Jesus's feet, when he seemed unresponsive. Jesus applauded her persistence (Matthew 15:21–28; Mark 7:24–30).

Other people who were suffering were more tentative, maybe even conflicted, in the ways they reached out to Jesus. The woman with the flow of blood just touched the hem of Jesus's garment (Matthew 9:18–26; Mark 5:25–34; Luke 8:43–48); the man with the withered hand didn't approach Jesus for healing, but when Jesus told him to hold out his hand, he did (Matthew 12:9–15; Mark 3:1–6); the father of the possessed boy—speaking for us all—cried out, "I believe; help my unbelief!" (Mark 9:24). Perhaps they were tentative in their approach because they had experienced discrimination from their communities and from religious leaders, as has been the experience of so many afflicted with HIV.

Some suffering people didn't ask for Jesus's response, but he responded to their affliction nevertheless. The Gerasene demoniac begged Jesus not to torment him, but Jesus healed him anyway (Mark 5:1–20). Some were so trapped in pain and chronic suffering that they didn't ask him for help, but he helped them. The widow of Nain, who had lost her only son, received Jesus's compassion without asking for it (Luke 7:11–17); and the paralytic at the pool of Bethesda was healed even though he was so blinded by suffering that he couldn't tell Jesus what he wanted (John 5:1–13). All these people bore afflictions similar to those borne by people affected by the HIV epidemic. Jesus didn't respond to them with judgment, moral lessons, talk of deferred hope, or existential harmony. He attended to the real people in their real circumstances.

Stay Awake, Be Watchful, Pray

Jesus serves as our exemplar in affliction: in caring for those who are afflicted, and in the experience of our own suffering. Jesus bore affliction. He suffered physically. In Gethsemane he bled, sweated, and wept. He suffered the disintegration of his company of followers, and he was denied, betrayed, and abandoned. He said to his friends, "'My soul is overwhelmed with sorrow to the point of death. Stay here and keep watch with me'" (Matthew 26:38, NIV). He agonized in solitude, and, like Martha from Africa, he cried out to God.

There is no experience of suffering we cannot share with our God that God has not experienced. In attending to those who suffer, we can take our cue from what Jesus asked of his disciples as he agonized in Gethsemane: stay awake; be watchful; pray (Luke 22:39–46; Mark 14:32–42; Matthew 26:36–46).

Suffering is frightening. In our fear we are tempted to primal responses of fleeing, sleeping, freezing, turning away—and we use our minds to try and figure things out and fix them. Nothing is necessarily wrong with these responses to fearful circumstances. But we are called to look at—stay awake to—the reality of suffering. For those of us who do not visit Africa or live in the vicinities where the HIV pandemic is raging, it is much too easy to close our eyes. Yet, a person bearing the weight of this infection may be sitting right next to us in the pew, just as Martha worships weekly beside people who don't know her story.

Jesus told his friends he was sorrowful unto death. How hard that must have been for them to hear. Yet he asked them to face the whole of his experience. We, too, are not only to stay awake to those who suffer; we are to be watchful and bear witness to the particular experiences of particular persons, as best we can. Those particulars that reside in larger conditions and situations inform how we direct our attention, and being watchful includes that social, medical, and political knowledge. And watchfulness attends to the more intimate human experiences, as well. The sorrow. Tears. The breaking heart. The beauty of faith. Courage. All of it.

It is in turning toward God in the midst of suffering that we may experience consolation and hope. Martha still attends church, even though the churches she has attended have not responded helpfully to the HIV crisis, nor have they been places of safe openness about her affliction. Her son told one pastor about his illness, and after that the pastor avoided him: "That was the end of it," according to Martha. The church is, however, a place where she prays. She has prayed for herself and her son, and she prays for those to whom she ministers. In prayer we tell God about what we notice as we stay awake with those who suffer.

There are signs that God's grace is present in the HIV crisis. Some of those signs are on view in the stories told in this book. Others come to us from researchers and reporters. One hopeful report of Jesus's healing presence in the midst of the epidemic was recently reported by the press. Columbia University demographer James F. Phillips and African colleagues have published findings claiming to show that knowing the Jesus who listens to us in our suffering makes a difference in the lives of the Kassena-Nankana women who live in the Ghanaian hinterlands. Those who are converts to Christianity were three times as likely to use family planning as were their counterparts who adhered to traditional African faith. Traditionally, these women are not part of decision-making in the home or village, and they're forbidden to communicate with ancestors and other spiritual beings. Men make the decisions and engage in religious communication. But the women who have become Christians have learned of a God who wants to hear from them and also wants to listen to them. He may well be the first "male" they've encountered who does. The researchers believe that the experience of a male deity who listens to them may have empowered the women to have conversations with their husbands about such issues as family size, contraceptive use, immunizations for children, and more (Helen Epstein, "Talking Their Way Out of a Population Crisis," *New York Times*, 23 October, 2011, SR4). This is good news for the world, and specifically for those confronting HIV in Africa. In Christ, human suffering and future hope are joined, for God's dwelling place is among people. To all of this, we are called to bear witness.

Martha speaks to our God without fear. She doesn't speak to everyone in that way. There is so much we can learn from Martha and people like her. For these people to tell their stories, we need to be trustworthy, welcoming, compassionate. If we are not, we compound the suffering, adding insult to injury, and driving those affected into silence. Jesus listened with love to people who were suffering in silence, as are so many women with HIV today. We are invited to go and do likewise.

Additional Reading

Beya, Bernadette. "Women in the Church in Africa: Possibilities for Presence and Promises." In *Talitha Cum! Theologies of African Women*, edited by Nyambura J. Njoroge and Musa W. Dube. Pietermaritzburg, SA: Cluster, 2001.

Farley, Wendy. *Tragic Vision, Divine Compassion: A Contemporary Theodicy*. Louisville: Westminster John Knox, 1990.

Hunter, Mark. *Love in the Time of AIDS: Inequality, Gender, and Rights in South Africa*. Bloomington: Indiana University Press, 2010.

Iliffe, John. *The African AIDS Epidemic: A History*. Oxford: Currey, 2006.

Mageto, Peter. *Victim Theology: A Critical Look at the Church's Response to AIDS*. Bloomington, IN: AuthorHouse, 2006.

Nolan, Stephanie. *28: Stories of AIDS in Africa*. New York: Walker, 2007.

Panichas, George A., editor. *The Simone Weil Reader*. New York: McKay, 1977.

Soelle, Dorothee. *Suffering*. Translated by Everett R. Kalin. Philadelphia: Fortress, 1975.

9

Women as Compassionate Champions
The Doers and the Leaders

NYAMBURA J. NJOROGE

A Rich Legacy of Women Doers and Leaders

AFTER THIRTY YEARS WITH the global HIV pandemic, there are many lessons we have learned from people living with HIV—including children born with the virus and those who deeply care for people who have been afflicted by HIV-related stigma, discrimination, and illnesses. In sub-Saharan Africa, the Joint United Nations Programme on HIV and AIDS (UNAIDS) has documented that 60% of all people living with HIV are women, especially young women of childbearing age. It is also a well-known fact that women make up the majority of caregivers for children and the sick as well as the majority of resource-providers—even though the latter is rarely highlighted because men are believed or expected to be the "breadwinners." In Africa, a large percentage of the women living with HIV and providing much-needed care and resources happen to be women of faith, among them Christian women from a very wide range of Christian traditions and denominations. These women also come from a huge variety of social stratifications, cultural differences, races, languages, levels of education, professions, political affiliations, and economic statuses.

In my work with Ecumenical HIV and AIDS Initiative in Africa (EHAIA), a ministry of the World Council of Churches (WCC), I have interacted with many women living with HIV who are still caregivers and providers, whom I commonly refer to as "compassionate champions: the doers and leaders." I have discovered the invaluable and unprecedented leadership that Christian women in Africa provide in the ecumenical response to the global HIV pandemic in the churches, theological institutions, and local communities. Women of faith have been at the frontlines in the battle against the HIV pandemic despite being consistently under-resourced and marginalized in the decision- and policymaking mechanisms of their religious communities. Because church leadership in Africa is predominately male and hierarchical, Christian women's leadership in the HIV response is mostly acknowledged in passing, sometimes trivialized, and often poorly documented. Sadly, this lack of acknowledgment is not unique to the handling of the HIV crisis. One has to dig deep into the Bible and church history books to find accounts of the women who should be serving as our modern-day role models and mentors, and whom we should celebrate as leaders and theologians.

In this chapter, I will demonstrate how our theological institutions and the global Church can move forward in handling the crisis of HIV by building on the monumental contributions and strengths of Christian women in sub-Saharan Africa despite, or perhaps because of, seemingly insurmountable challenges. I will start the discussion with a woman from the gospels to demonstrate that women of faith—and Christian faith, in particular—belong to a rich legacy of compassionate champions. This example and others that follow are worth emulating and building on as we continue to confront the HIV pandemic.

A Story of Forgiveness and Loving-Kindness

For reasons I am still exploring, I feel empowered by the narrative of the woman who anointed Jesus. Hers is a legacy I wish all Christian leaders would seek to embody. Her story is found in all four gospels, albeit with varying details: Matthew 26:6–13; Mark 14:3–9; Luke 7:36–50; and John 12:1–8. Except for John, who refers to her as Mary, the sister of Lazarus and Martha, the synoptic gospels leave her nameless. The gospel of John refers to Lazarus as one of those reclining at the table with Jesus, while Martha serves. Mark and Matthew identify the host as Simon the Leper, and Luke calls him Simon the Pharisee. According to Matthew, Mark, and John, the event takes place in Bethany close to the time of the Passover feast. Significantly, the incident takes place at dinner, and the nameless woman is most certainly not on the guest list. However, Luke fashions the account with some rather embarrassing and elaborate details: a woman from the city starts weeping and wiping Jesus's feet with tears, kissing and anointing them. She did not dare ask to come in or even seek permission from Jesus to perform her intimate gesture. In today's assessment, she could well be accused of sexual harassment. She just throws herself on the floor and gets lost in "the act," to the annoyance of the host and other guests.

Despite the variations, in all of the gospels, someone in the room seems uncomfortable or disgusted with what they witness, and they cannot hold back. They feel obliged to speak their mind, but the woman remains silent. She does not waste time explaining herself and the reason she is convinced that she needs to anoint Jesus in the manner that she does. She acts in the way that she believes she needs to. Jesus seems to be pleased by the surprise interruption and emphatically directs the disgusted men to "leave her alone."

In Luke's version, Jesus takes the opportunity to challenge Simon's judgmental thoughts with truth about how God chooses to respond to those who repent, though they have "many sins"—with the gifts of forgiveness, loving-kindness, and peace. Yet there were people at the table who still do not understand his identity—"Who is this who even forgives sins?" (Luke 7:49b)—especially because Jesus allows himself to be anointed by a scorned and stigmatized woman. In the Hebrew society, the anointing of prophets, priests, and kings was done by men, for men. It therefore does not surprise me that we hardly ever hear sermons on this particular incident in our churches, even though, in the Johannian account, Jesus said that this woman will be remembered anytime the Gospel is preached. I recall doing precisely that—remembering this woman in a sermon in an ecumenical setting. Sometime later, an Anglican priest (I am a Presbyterian minister) confronted and rebuked me for emphasizing that the woman anointed Jesus! Today, I revisit this text: What does this narrative say to us in the era of HIV?

Age-Old Sin: The Big Lie about Women

In this age and in the context of HIV, which is primarily sexually transmitted, we in communities of faith are quick to associate HIV-infected status with sexual immorality. Therefore, being HIV-infected translates into punishment from God because of sexual sins. As a result, there are Christians (even, and perhaps especially, Christian leaders) who, after thirty years with HIV, cannot bring themselves to identify with other people living with HIV—especially if these other people living with HIV happen to be Christian women. In my view, despite the distance in time and the social and religious-cultural differences, this powerful narrative of the woman who anointed Jesus speaks volumes to our HIV context. Her story is one that sheds light upon inequality between women and men that promotes ruthless and harsh judgment toward women, stigma, silencing, shame, discrimination, rejection, blaming, and demonizing: it is age-old sin that Jesus faced squarely and condemned in his teachings.

Needless to say, narratives of women and their sexual lifestyles and/or marriage statuses provoked insightful discourse in the gospels (e.g., John 4:1–42; 8:1–11). Yet it is taking Christians in Africa such a long time to recognize and confront judgmental and stigmatizing attitudes against women in various social situations (childless women, widows, unmarried women, single mothers, divorced women) let alone the stigma and discrimination against people living with disability and now people living with HIV. The list seems to keep on growing. Gender disparity is an age-old sin that churches have lagged behind in addressing, despite our claim that women and men are created equal in the likeness of God (Genesis 1:26–27) and that we are the salt and light of the world (Matthew 5:13–14). But most importantly for our purposes in this chapter, the woman who anointed Jesus demonstrates how women sometimes respond and assert their God-given dignity and rights in hostile and disempowering environments. This is one lesson we should take with us from this powerful narrative. Irrespective of what some of the men in the room thought and said about the woman, she knew her place in the presence of Jesus, who affirmed her full humanity and her prophetic action.

So rather than engage in endless debates about their role and place in leadership, some women simply act and do what needs to be done. For instance, in the gospels we encounter other women who followed, learned from, and served Jesus, ultimately becoming part of God's prophetic mission. In her thought-provoking book *In Memory of Her*, Elisabeth Schüssler Fiorenza reminds us that women were true disciples of Jesus who followed and ministered to him, even to the bitter end on the cross. Women disciples, unlike many of the men disciples, stayed with Jesus at the hour of his greatest need. It does not surprise me, therefore, that they were the first to discover that Jesus had risen from the tomb.

Then and now, women have been at the frontlines of God's prophetic mission whether they are acknowledged by the male leadership or not. But it is deplorable that it takes something as horrific as the HIV pandemic to remind Christians that God abhors gender discrimination and judgmental and stigmatizing stances toward anyone. Ironically, it is generally people living with HIV—the ones most affected—who candidly share their experiences, which have opened our eyes and ears and deepened our awareness to the fact that stigma and discrimination are sins against God.

Today we know that the sins of stigma, shame, discrimination, denial, inaction, and misaction have caused great pain, ongoing suffering, and unthinkable loss. In other words, in addressing the HIV pandemic, we reveal many sins and begin to see what is wrong in our lives, in our societies, and even in our communities of faith—especially to the extent that we disrespect and dehumanize women. On the other hand, HIV has revealed the great courage, unwavering faith, resolute resilience, abundant compassion, patient endurance, and stubborn hope of the most affected people in Africa, especially children, youth, and women.

In Her Legacy: Exceptional Leadership

Knowingly or unknowingly, many African women (not exclusively Christian) have acted like the woman who anointed Jesus by revealing God's powerful forgiveness, loving-kindness, and peace. African women have demonstrated great wisdom and generosity as they have stepped out to take care of themselves and entire families in very difficult and trying times, facing the HIV pandemic, endemic sex- and gender-based violence, hunger, ethnic conflicts, wars, and even genocide. It is no exaggeration that, when war breaks out and men take up arms—including the use of rape as weapon of war—it is women who are left to serve the families, the children (unfortunately today some are recruited as child soldiers), the injured, the sick, and the elderly with few or no resources at their disposal. So even as we focus on the HIV pandemic, it is noteworthy that African women throughout the continent have much more than the HIV pandemic to contend with.

To illustrate, in a powerful memoir, *Mighty Be Our Powers: How Sisterhood, Prayer, and Sex Changed a Nation at War,* Leymah Gbowee (2011 Nobel Peace Prize Laureate from Liberia) narrates how in 2003 she and other women in Liberia helped organize and lead the Liberian Mass Action for Peace, a coalition of Christian and Muslim women who sat in public protest, confronting a ruthless president and rebel warlords. Like the woman who anointed Jesus, Gbowee did not wait to be invited to the peace talks, nor did she seek for anyone's permission to act; but without her exceptional servant leadership, Liberia could well be at war as I write.

Similarly, the "war" against the HIV pandemic has created huge burdens for women. As the most infected and affected, women have organized and led support groups that have nurtured children and people living with HIV without discrimination. For instance, in Kenya, Asunta Wagura, who has been HIV-infected for almost twenty-five years, has reached out to thousands of women (and some men) living with HIV through the Kenya Network of Women with HIV (KENWA—over 10,000 members), which she cofounded in 1993. She is currently the chief executive officer, and she has also adopted three children and is a mother of three boys, all HIV-uninfected. Even though KENWA is a community-initiated organization, because most Kenyans and especially women practice their faith, I imagine the majority of the members belong to a religious community where they impact others with what they learn from one another. Wagura herself does not shy away from identifying with God: "I draw my strength from the fact that God created each one of us in his own image; I'm not worth less than anyone. HIV does not mean I'm created in the 'image' of a virus! God's plan for my life was not altered because of this virus. I have courage, because my life is not a rehearsal. I feel I must live a fulfilled life like anyone else, without regrets or apologies or explanations to justify failure! I have a right to be here" (http://wwww.kenyanmagazines.com/asunta-wagura/).

Wagura's work has been featured by CNN International on the "African Voices" program. Her story, like those of so many others, needs to be shared so that we may all be inspired and learn how to help those around us. KENWA has plans of spreading to South Sudan. Other organizations have taken in orphans and groups of people made vulnerable through HIV and nurtured them to wholeness. A campaign for grandmothers in the era of HIV has been promoted by Stephen Lewis (http://www.stephenlewisfoundation.org/get-involved/grandmothers-campaign). Other stories abound.

Women have served the sick and the dying with exceptional merit and have demonstrated exceptional servant leadership despite unthinkable suffering and loss. According to Jesus, true leadership is servant leadership—which he demonstrated by washing the feet of the disciples before the Passover meal. In my view, it is no accident that, in the gospel of John, the narrative of Mary anointing Jesus's feet precedes the narrative of Jesus's washing the feet of the disciples (John 12–13). Could Jesus have gotten the idea of footwashing from Mary? Why not?

In the gospels, there is no ambiguity. Women are equally called and endowed by the Holy Spirit to carry out servant leadership and to participate in God's prophetic mission in a wide variety of ministries, contrary to what many churches teach and preach. In Christ, women enjoy full humanity despite the big lie that has been propagated, in many ways, that women are inferior to men. Unfortunately, churches continue to teach that men are the head of the family, even when large percentages of African families are single-handedly managed and led by single women. And in many other families, where husbands and fathers are present, women work alongside the men: Oftentimes the women are the sole breadwinners, in addition to managing their households. It is therefore no surprise that churches in Africa, which are packed with women as the majority of followers, depend on the generosity and service of women, even though they are denied their rightful place at the "dinner table" of ecclesiastical leadership and decision- and policy-making.

Women and Men Working in Partnership

Excluding women from leadership at all levels weakens the commitment and contributions of churches, theological institutions, and the global Church in their participation in God's prophetic mission. It translates to women's priorities and specific needs' being inadequately articulated and under-resourced. For instance, matters of sexuality, reproductive health education and justice are hardly ever discussed in churches or theological institutions except when governments want to legalize abortion. Similarly, little attention is given to maternal health care despite the high rates of ma- ternal death and infant mortality in Africa. Yet 40 to 70 percent of health care in many African countries is provided by churches and other religious communities. Whenever human life is threatened, churches need to ac- tively discover what is wrong and what should be done, and, if necessary, lobby the governments for better protection for their citizens—especially children. It is not enough for churches to focus on baptizing children, bless- ing them, and welcoming them into the house of God when they neglect to care for their well-being from the time they are in their mothers' wombs, especially now that so many children are born HIV-infected. Responsible and healthy sexuality, childbearing, and parenting are matters that require full engagement of both women and men, and the churches should be at the forefront of providing much-needed education.

At this juncture, it is noteworthy that, twenty years into the HIV pandemic, UNAIDS has created a campaign to get men meaningfully engaged in confronting the HIV pandemic—a clear indication that, to a large extent, women have been left to shoulder the burden of the times: preventing HIV transmission, facing HIV-related stigma, handling deaths, and addressing the myriad other adverse impacts that the HIV pandemic has created. Similarly, in the Circle of Concerned African Women Theologians (hereafter, the Circle), of which this author is a founding member, women have provided leadership in naming theological, ethical, cultural, and religious beliefs, as well as harmful practices and leadership styles, that fuel gender disparity, social injustices, and the spread of HIV in religious communities and in society at large. Additionally, the Circle has endeavored to provide theological and ethical reflections that are empowering and transformative to the behaviors contrary to God's will for how women and men relate to each other in families, religious contexts, and everyday life.

To some extent, the Circle has been instrumental in transforming ecumenical theological education and ministerial training in Africa, which has been "reserved" for men over the centuries. Through the Circle, women theologians have participated in creating and growing a theological platform that provides safe space for women to voice their experiences and insightful theological and ethical perspectives. Women have spoken truth to themselves and to those in power in the churches and theological institutions: They have stated that women are not powerless and passive victims, as usually depicted. Rather like men, they acknowledge they are powerfully, wonderfully, and fearfully created in the image and likeness of God (Psalm 139). In other words, here women have demonstrated, in word and deed, that they are not inferior to men, and they assert their God-given right to be fully human.

Through Circle-related events, women theologians have challenged men to engage in deep theological conversations concerning what it means to be women and men created in the likeness of God. For instance, through in-depth scrutiny of the scriptures and of indigenous African cultures and religions, together with men, women scholars and activists have addressed endemic sex- and gender-based violence and its link to the HIV pandemic. This is occurring to the point where men are now questioning masculinity and "father wound" (i.e., growing up not knowing who your father is).

Some of these studies were unheard of a decade ago. By effecting these discussions and thought processes, women in Africa are also identifying how they themselves participate in "training" men to believe that they (the men) are superior to women—being the protectors and breadwinners, among other gender-based stereotypes that put men on pedestals. It is important to point out, however, that this kind of partnership—of women and men theologically questioning gender dynamics together—is in its infancy. Many crucial issues have yet to be discussed—for instance, child marriages, incest, and sexual violence (including marital rape) that occurs in many societies, with churches remaining disturbingly silent.

Speaking the Truth to Us:
Hearing Stories from Our Bellies (from Our Hearts)

It is important to emphasize that, for women to take their rightful place at the front lines in overcoming social injustices that fuel gender disparity, the HIV pandemic, endemic sex- and gender-based violence, ethnic conflicts, wars, genocide, hunger, and bad leadership, they have to speak the truth to themselves (i.e., overcome their internalized inferiority complex) long before they speak truth to those in power and to the male leadership. Women have to say no to age-old lies perpetuated by religious communities and societies at large about women and leadership. In her memoir, Leymah Gbowee recalls a time when she created a safe place for women to share their stories. After many painful narratives, she felt that they could not go on. But an elderly woman with her walking stick implored, "The UN brings us food and shelter and clothes, but what you've brought is much more valuable. You've come to hear the stories from our bellies. Stories that no one else asks us about. Please, don't stop. Don't ever stop."

Listening to these stories from the bellies of the women devastated by war empowered Gbowee and her small group of women leaders to strategize and plan how they were going to demand peace. Even though she doubted her suitability (many women do) as a leader for Christian (Lutheran) women because, by her own confession, she was "drinking too much and fornicating," God continued to guide her, and she became the leader Liberia needed at the time. Prayer became her number-one strategy, and the rest is "her story!" In the quest for peace, the women discovered truth about themselves and about their country, and about what they could do to make a difference. Gbowee's account is repeated countless times, in manifold ways, through the lives of women living with HIV and through those most affected in Africa as people demand to live and to have life in abundance in a continent devastated by many woes. I believe Jesus focuses on women's courage and faith in God rather than on their "many sins," just as he did with the woman at Simon's house.

Taking a cue from these Liberian women, we learn that facing the truth about ourselves empowers us as we seek God's gifts—peace, forgiveness, reconciliation with God and with one another, and much-needed healing for what too often happens behind the scenes in the churches in Africa—human failure, leadership failure, the many secrets of incest and sexual violence in Christian homes, as well as failure to accept the HIV-infected status of Christians. As much as I appreciate and see the need to speak the truth to those in power, as in the political arena, I am convinced that, unless people of faith speak the truth to ourselves *first*, our credibility is at stake because, as Christians, we have neglected to heed the Gospel calling for servant leadership. The hallmarks of servant leadership—humility, courage, compassion, patient endurance, resilience, wisdom, faith, hope, and loving-kindness—do not just pop up out of nowhere. Building this kind of leadership involves a process of soul-searching and hard work that demands questioning why things have gone so wrong and what we can do, individually and as communities of faith, to effect change and to transform our societies. One testimony of such deep work is *The Sacrifice of Africa,* where Emmanuel Katongole gives illustrations of what it takes to be a servant and effective leader in war- and HIV-stricken African contexts.

Creating Safe Spaces for Questioning Scriptures

Fortunately, through programs like EHAIA, Africans are creating safe spaces through contextual Bible study methodology workshops on texts that help us to explore the HIV pandemic, sex- and gender-based violence, gender disparity, and leadership. These workshops address insecurity, intimidation, judgmental lifestyles, stigma, shame, discrimination, denial, inaction, and misaction to the point where participants experience honesty and empowerment that is rarely encountered via everyday liturgies and sermons. In these safe spaces, women who have been sexually abused or who have experienced child marriage, for instance, speak out and share horror stories (from their bellies), working towards healing, forgiveness, and reconciliation. For some time, primarily women have participated in many of these workshops; however, now more men are participating, asking difficult questions such as why some men rape, and why families marry their very young daughters to older men (sometimes old enough to be their grandfathers). Consequently, both women and men are intensively questioning African masculinity and the notion of manhood, as well as femininity and the concept of womanhood, in the Christian milieu. Male biblical characters are closely studied as men seek worthy role models. Even men in high-ranking leadership positions are slowly beginning to acknowledge that they, too, need safe spaces to ponder how they lead and how they can transform hierarchical and patriarchal styles that are disempowering and that do not practice servant leadership.

Furthermore, there is growing appreciation that this gender-focused discourse is not an enclave reserved for women, but rather that both women and men are engaging one another in conversation—even though each sex (and also each generation-specific group) may need its own space at certain times. The contextual Bible study methodology encourages intensive, inclusive participation by engaging biblical texts carefully selected to allow focus on certain topics, as well as on certain social and cultural factors. Some biblical scholars are also exploring how to do contextual Bible studies with children, given that they, too, are subjected to sexual abuse and harmful cultural practices. It is clear that there are many obstacles to overcome, particularly in addressing issues of leadership; but we know that without righteous and courageous leadership, Africa is doomed. Many Christians in Africa (and elsewhere) have come to realize that engaging the Bible during worship and daily reading at home is not enough, so contextual Bible study workshops are in high demand as word spreads about the effectiveness of the methodology. Scholars and HIV program officers are also embarking on projects such as authoring books and manuals on emerging topics such as masculinity and how to raise children who respect the humanity of women and men equally.

Conclusion: Learning from Her Story

In this chapter, I have attempted to expound lessons that we can learn from the generous, courageous, and prophetic act performed by a woman who, in the eyes of some, did not deserve to be in the presence of Jesus, let alone touch him. Taking cues from her story, I have tried to demonstrate that, in this era of the HIV pandemic and endemic violence, African Christian women, knowingly or unknowingly, have built on this powerful legacy of a woman who did not shy away from doing what she believed was the right thing to do. Furthermore, in his own way, Jesus teaches us not to focus on the weaknesses (including sins) of the individual, but on their strengths. Jesus concentrates on the courage, faith, and kindness of the very woman that he acknowledges has many sins. Certainly, there are still people who wonder if anything good can come from Africa and, in particular, from its "poor," disempowered, and silenced women.

But women in Africa have narrated their story—*her* story—not so much in word, but in deed as they stand in the way of rape, of child marriage, of marital rape that brings HIV to their bodies and to the bodies of their unborn children. Women in Africa have shared the painful stories from their bellies—discovering their HIV-positive status, shame and stigma (self and social), discrimination and rejection that come with this new condition. Women have named their unthinkable suffering and loss. Equally important, they have embarked on the journey of long-term prevention of sexual violence and HIV transmission, and they have nursed the sick and fed the orphans.

Furthermore, women are engaged biblically and theologically with matters of life and death. They have called men and the male-dominated church leadership to be accountable for their own behavior and for actions that keep HIV spreading and keep women silenced. In particular, women from all walks of life are challenging men to be fully involved in ending HIV transmission, gender disparity, sex- and gender-based violence, child marriages, and other harmful cultural practices—which are largely responsible for the problems in many families and in the lives of children and women. Women want churches, theological institutions, and the global Church to ensure that women are included in all decision- and policy-making bodies, and that issues such as sexuality, sexual reproductive health, education, justice, maternal health, and child mortality are well-placed in the discussions and budgets. Despite of, or because of, insurmountable problems and challenges, women in Africa have learned to survive and to manage with limited resources, but that is not to say that they are self-sufficient. African women need friends (not handouts) from far and near to build and nurture collaborative partnerships across countries and continents, so that God's prophetic mission to end the HIV pandemic, stigma, discrimination, endemic violence, and untimely deaths will be accomplished in Africa and elsewhere. Therefore, let us preach the Gospel of Jesus Christ and tell her story!

Additional Reading

Dube, Musa Wenkosi. *The HIV & AIDS Bible: Selected Essays*. Scranton: University of Scranton Press, 2008.

Gbowee, Leymah, with Carol Mithers. *Mighty Be Our Powers: How Sisterhood, Prayer, and Sex Changed a Nation at War: A Memoir*. New York: Beast Books, 2011.

Katongole, Emmanuel. *The Sacrifice of Africa: A Political Theology for Africa*. Grand Rapids: Eerdmans, 2011.

Kelly, Michael J. *HIV and AIDS: A Social Justice Perspective*. Nairobi: Paulines Publications Africa, 2010.

McKenna, Megan. *Leave Her Alone*. Maryknoll, NY: Orbis, 2000.

———. *Not Counting Women and Children: Neglected Stories from the Bible*. Maryknoll, NY: Orbis, 1994.

Schüssler Fiorenza, Elisabeth. *In Memory of Her: A Feminist Theological Reconstruction of Christian Origins*. New York: Crossroad, 1989.

WCC/EHAIA Series Publications. Online: http://www.oikoumene.org/en/programmes/justice-diakonia-and-responsibility-for-creation/hivaids-initiative-in-africa-ehaia/documents.html#c24280.

10

Stories from Women with HIV

ERIKA NOSSOKOFF & ARTHUR J. AMMANN

Introduction

THERE ARE MANY STORIES that women who are infected with HIV tell. Most of these are hidden within a small community, usually composed of other HIV-infected women, who share in their struggles to overcome a chronic and often fatal disease that overshadows every part of their daily lives. They suffer not only the consequences of HIV infection, a chronic and debilitating disease, but too often, the stigma and discrimination that accompany a diagnosis of HIV infection. They find comfort among one another as they seek spiritual strength from their strong belief that God provides for those who are in pain and who are suffering, no matter the cause. Often, unlike other diseases, such as cancer or diabetes, they are not free to share their struggle with HIV with others in the Christian community, including their own churches, for fear of discrimination, and so they suffer in silence with the consequences of HIV infection and what it has done to themselves, their families, and their children. Their fear of how the Christian community will respond denies them refuge that has been promised to all in Christ, and it denies the Christian community the opportunity to be blessed by acting out the compassion taught by Jesus.

We provide two stories from women who are HIV-infected. They live in different countries, and, although their personal experiences differ markedly in their response to HIV, they have in common HIV infection and the universal cry for spiritual help and comfort.

Names and locations have been changed to protect confidentiality.

The Story of Martha (As told by Arthur J. Ammann)

The last time I saw Martha was twelve years ago. The circumstances were not encouraging. At that time, I was consulting with Ann Petru, MD, a pediatric infectious disease specialist in the HIV clinic. Martha was at Children's Hospital in Oakland, California, because, two months after arriving in the United States from Sub-Saharan Africa, her infant son had become critically ill with severe diarrhea and weight loss. After her husband died in Africa from an undiagnosed illness, a friend invited her to come to America to help her recover from her loss.

When I saw Martha and her son, he was critically ill and close to death. It was then that I heard of the death of her husband and her firstborn child. I was almost certain that HIV lay behind these tragic events. In all likelihood, HIV had sown its thread of infection from husband to wife, to children, and now was threatening the life of this, their last young son who lay before us.

Emergency treatment was provided, and, weeks later, the diagnosis of HIV infection was confirmed—first in the critically ill child, and then in his mother. Martha was not eager to be tested, but, after an explanation of what HIV could do, and after learning that there was treatment to prevent complications, she agreed. It was then that treatment with antiretroviral drugs was initiated. At that time, there were far fewer drugs than the now thirty drugs and combinations of drugs to treat HIV infection, so neither Dr. Petru nor I was certain that the drugs could reverse the damage that HIV had done. Thankfully, the drugs worked, and slowly the ravages of the infection were reversed. What became clear then was that Martha and her son had to stay in the U.S. in order to continue to get the lifesaving drugs. Going back to Sub-Saharan Africa, where no drugs were available, would have been a death sentence.

I was asked to write a letter of support to the immigration service stating that Martha and her child had to stay in the U.S. in order to continue to have access to the antiretroviral drugs that were keeping them alive. Fortunately, with the help of a pro bono lawyer, the immigration service agreed.

Shortly afterwards, I lost contact with Martha and her child, and now, twelve years later, I considered the remote possibility that she and her son might still be alive—but in what health? I was working on a project of the impact of HIV on women and their families, and I wanted to contact Martha to see what had happened to both of them over the twelve years of their stay in the U.S., or to know whether or not they had returned to Sub-Saharan Africa. Were they well, or were they in advanced stages of AIDS? Had the treatment continued to work? Were they on more advanced drugs?

I took a chance and called Martha using the only phone number that I had in my database—one that was twelve years old. The phone rang several times, and then a quiet voice said, "Hello."

"Is this Martha" I asked? "I saw you twelve years ago at the Children's Hospital." Within a short period of time, I found out not only that she was healthy, but her son was alive. I then asked if we could visit her and learn more about what had happened during the twelve years that had elapsed since I last saw her. One week later, we made our way to her home. With me was Susan Phillips, Executive Director of New College Berkeley, who was writing an essay on the pain and suffering of people with HIV and wanted to hear firsthand what some of the women with HIV endure.

We knocked at the door of a tiny apartment in downtown Hayward. Martha herself opened the door. I looked at her. I was somewhat startled. I was not used to seeing women who have HIV so healthy and cheerful. As we walked down the narrow hallway into the small living room, her son opened up the door to his room. Out stepped a tall, handsome young man who had journeyed from Sub-Saharan Africa as a baby, had come close to dying at that young age, and now to stood before us healthy and eager to start his high school education.

Martha was quick to relay to us that she was now in school preparing to earn a community public health degree so that she could help individuals access health care. Treatment had indeed made the difference. Drugs were now so potent that a single pill needed to be taken only once a day to reverse the devastating effects of the virus and to keep the virus in check. Had she returned to her own country twelve years ago, neither Martha nor her son would be alive. With treatment, both mother and son were healthy—providing Martha with a normal life and preventing her son from being added to the list of 15 million HIV orphans. I thought to myself, "If only these medicines were available to all of the women of Sub-Saharan Africa who would then be healthy enough to care for their families, keep their babies from becoming infected with HIV, and prevent their children from becoming orphans."

During the interview, we talked about the attitude of friends and neighbors toward HIV in Sub-Saharan Africa at the time that she left more than a decade ago. There was much superstition. HIV was felt by many to be a disease that the witch doctors induced, and when Martha's husband died, and then her daughter, her family felt that she might have had a role in their illnesses. There was no mention of HIV, and no thought that her husband might have been responsible for his own death and that of his daughter.

Martha told us that her husband's HIV infection was most likely acquired during his travels. He was a man who worked for a large corporation in Africa, successful enough to live a middle-class life and to travel to Europe to conduct business. Martha had heard of two women who her husband knew, each one in a different country, who had died of AIDS. In all likelihood, they had acquired it from her husband. HIV infection had traveled with him back to Sub-Saharan Africa, and before he showed any signs of illness, he had transmitted the virus to her. Martha knew nothing about either his or her own infection, and she could therefore do nothing to prevent her children from becoming infected with HIV. Her first child, a girl, died suddenly in Sub-Saharan Africa. In retrospect, she probably died of HIV infection. Her husband became progressively more and more ill, and he died after Martha gave birth to a boy, her second child. Following his death, she had decided to come to America with her son at the invitation of a friend who knew nothing about HIV infection.

Martha told us that she had very little anger toward her husband. When we probed, she acknowledged that initially she felt some anger, but now, more than a decade later, she expressed forgiveness, because "he died of HIV while I received treatment, and now I am healthy and caring for others who are sick."

"How do you think the HIV epidemic will stop?" we asked. She had no clear answer, but she did acknowledge that men had a primary role in infecting women. The reluctance of men to be tested—or to even admit that, because they had multiple sexual partners, they were at risk for HIV—was and continues to be a major obstacle to women's learning about infection before they become sick or before they can protect themselves from infection. Some men, even if they know they are infected, refuse to tell their wives or to use condoms to protect their wives, and, in turn, to protect their children from the consequences of HIV.

Several years ago, Martha returned to her country. She had started a nonprofit organization to assist widows and orphans in Sub-Saharan Africa who were the victims of the HIV epidemic. Once there, she spoke with the country's first lady, who subsequently came to the United States to participate in a fundraiser for Martha's nonprofit organization. Martha now talks to people about being infected and about how they need to take care of themselves. She gets companies to donate funds and supplies to help hospitals. Martha feels that now in Sub-Saharan Africa, all churches are helping.

Much had changed between the time she first left Africa and her return visit. Twelve years ago, HIV was not acknowledged in Sub-Saharan Africa, nor was it discussed openly. There was no treatment, and anyone who was infected was likely to die within five or six years. Now, people are talking about HIV more openly. Medicines are still in short supply, but they are increasingly available. The Catholic Church is active in caring for orphans, and some churches provide help for widows with HIV. But on the whole, when Martha visited her home country, she discovered that stigma persisted. During her visit, Martha never revealed to anyone that she herself was HIV-infected.

We continued the interview. "Over the twelve years that you knew you were infected but getting treatment, what kind of help did you get from individuals, the community, or the church?" Martha remained silent for a moment. She then explained that most of the help came from women who, like herself, were HIV-infected and who had children that were also infected. They met and talked with one another to share experiences and to share where they could get help to cope with the many problems that a chronic infection precipitated. There were social workers that could help to get housing and food, and to get prescription drugs that might be too expensive to purchase on a limited income. Almost all of the funds came from the Children's Hospital Infectious Disease Team.

A surprise came to us when we asked whether Martha had gotten any help from the church she was attending. There was yet another, much longer pause. The church she was attending provided her with spiritual strength as she worshiped each Sunday and communicated with God in the holiness of the sanctuary. But in all the many years of attending the church, she never told anyone—parishioners, friends, not even the pastor—that she was infected with HIV. It was too great of a risk, and she knew that the most likely outcome would be stigma, something that she did not want to experience for either herself or her son. Thus—unlike other conditions such as cancer, diabetes, or stroke, where prayers were offered for those who suffered from disease—Martha suffered alone.

"What would you do if you were pastor?" I asked. Martha replied, "I would tell them that we are all a Christian family, and that HIV-infected women should be able to come to the pastor, too, and expect confidentiality, and that the pastor should be able to get the trust of the people to accept those who are HIV-infected with love and forgiveness. It could happen."

Martha had reason to believe that she and her son would be stigmatized. During his middle school years, her son had become aware of a church summer camp for children in the Hayward region. He desperately wanted to attend the church camp, and the pastor of the church seemed quite open to it. Her son felt an obligation to confide in the pastor that he was HIV-infected, feeling that it was something that those who ran the camp should know in case he became ill and needed medical help. The pastor promised that being HIV-infected would not make a difference, and that he would help get him to camp—but he never did.

Toward the end of the interview, I glanced around the room and saw photographs of what appeared to be many family members from Africa. I asked Martha if she could tell us who the people in the photographs were. Martha did not hesitate.

We began with a photograph on the far wall. It was of Martha and her husband before he became sick with AIDS. On another shelf was a photograph of her brother-in-law and his wife, both of whom died from HIV. There was also a photograph of their two children, a boy and a girl—the girl having died of AIDS while the boy was left orphaned. It was clear that HIV had invaded many families without anyone's confronting how HIV is spread, and without anyone's acting on the fact that it is a preventable infection.

At one point Martha said, "I asked God what he wanted me to do." We realized that, in spite of all the death and pain and suffering that she had experienced, and in spite of all of the discrimination that she had witnessed and feared, Martha continued to derive her strength from God, who directed her life. She was alive, she felt, because God wanted her to minister to others. She would continue to go to church and worship and talk to God alone, who provided her with the love and understanding that she needed. There in church, she would be surrounded by people who might not understand how far God's love reaches. They would be the ones who would miss out on the blessing of providing a refuge for the sick and suffering.

We ended by asking Martha, "With all that you've experienced, all the pain and suffering that you've endured, what would you like to do the most?" Martha replied, "What I want to do is save people's lives. If I can save one or two, that is what I want to do."

Rebecca: An HIV-infected Pastor
(As told by Erika Nossokoff)

"For we do not have a high priest who is unable to empathize with our weaknesses . . ." (Hebrews 4:15a).

Pastor Rebecca looked directly at the fifty or so Nigerian pastors and their wives. She had heard enough facts during this five-day "HIV and the Church" training in 2008; it was time to get personal. In her commanding yet friendly voice, she challenged her fellow pastors, "Will you marry a couple if you know that one or both of them are HIV-infected?"

Many of these religious leaders at the heart of African life squirmed in their white plastic chairs. The afternoon heat, fused with the question, caused some to sweat profusely. Anticipating their reluctance to answer honestly in the large group, Pastor Rebecca asked them to divide into smaller discussion groups. Ten members of the Faith Alive (a faith-based hospital and clinic) HIV-infected support group, not yet publicly identified, strategically blended into different groups.

Pastor Rebecca walked among the circles and heard many of the pastors and their wives say, "People with HIV are just going to die anyway. What is the use of getting married?" Others said, "It is their own fault that they are HIV-infected. They need to pay for their sins. We do not want those people in our churches infecting us."

Though not unexpected, their judgment stung. Pastor Rebecca steeled her tall, solid frame and glanced at a few of Faith Alive's support group members. Their brave silence about their own HIV infection strengthened her resolve to remain patient.

After allowing ample time for discussion, Pastor Rebecca gathered everyone back into one group. It was time for her to reveal the challenging truth. "Please, allow me to introduce a few of my friends," she said. "They are members of Faith Alive's weekly support group that I work with." She paused to intensify the moment. "All of them are HIV-infected. They are planning to marry or are newly married."

One by one, the very people who had, only moments before, sat next to and felt the unsympathetic hearts of many of the pastors and their wives came forward. Each support group member, nicely dressed and looking healthy, stood up and recounted painful stories of stigmatization and rejection by their Christian friends, families, pastors, and churches. Some had been thrown out of their homes or feared losing their jobs when others discovered that the virus flowed through their blood.

Yet each person talked about their future. Some talked about continuing their education at universities or through the Faith Alive computer, sewing, and knitting classes. Others worked in hospitals and schools. They hoped to start families and raise healthy children—now possible with medications that could stop the virus from infecting their babies during pregnancy and while breast-feeding.

"My first family is Faith Alive," one young woman said. "I am accepted there. Even on the days when my body feels sick, my spirit is strong. They have done for me what my own church has not."

As the support group members spoke, Pastor Rebecca watched the pastors' and their wives' eyes widen. Some dropped their jaws. Others looked down, too ashamed of the insensitive comments they had made just a few minutes earlier. Still others touched their faces, wiping fallen tears of shame and embarrassment.

Pastor Rebecca's patience was rewarded. No lecture could match the intensity of this lesson. Yet, she was not ready to reveal the whole truth: that she, a fellow pastor, also lived with HIV. Her story would have to wait until another time.

Eleven years earlier, in 1997, Rebecca extended her left hand toward the lab technician at Jos University Teaching Hospital during a prenatal visit. Her twenty-six-year-old body experienced the same tenderness and swelling as it had with her first two pregnancies. What differed was her tiredness from running after her boys, Kwemto and Chibuzo. She winced when the technician pricked her middle finger. Rebecca's blood flowed—it would be tested for HIV.

Afterward, Rebecca gathered her boys and left the hospital. They returned a few days later to collect the test results. The doctor told her that everything was fine. Perhaps he did not tell his patients about their HIV-infected status because there was no available treatment at that time.

Without treatment, HIV was a certain death sentence. Lifesaving antiret-roviral medications were too costly for even the wealthiest people then, let alone the wife of a construction worker whose out-of-town jobs only allowed him to sleep at home one or two nights a month.

But Rebecca sensed something in her doctor's voice that was not honest. Later, one of her friends who worked at that hospital visited Rebecca. The friend asked her if she wanted to know her blood test results. Yes. In her living room, with no counseling or advice about how to protect her baby, she learned the truth: She was infected with a virus called HIV.

Paralyzed by the reality of HIV, at first Rebecca did not hear the rain outside. It began to fall slowly, but soon pounded at the door like an uninvited visitor. So, too, had HIV entered her life and now indiscriminately saturated everything around her.

When her husband Azuka came home a few days later, she stopped weeping long enough to break the news. "It cannot be," he said. "There is no such thing as HIV." Unlike Rebecca, who did not doubt the virus, Azuka believed that this so-called disease was a curse from witch doctors rather than a consequence of his behavior.

"You cannot be serious," she said. The temporary comfort of denial tempted her, but the reality expanded like her body's pregnancy. "Well," she said, "we will see."

Neither the news of her status nor her pregnancy deterred Azuka's desire to have sexual relations with his wife, who still looked healthy. When he lay on top of her in their bedroom at night, she prayed. "God, take away my anger, and keep him away from other women. The children and I will need him now more than ever. You must be the one to work in his heart."

A few months later, they welcomed their new baby boy. They named him Testimony, because Rebecca knew that this boy would be proof of something. Exactly what, was yet to be seen. He seemed like a typical baby until about six or seven months later, when he started getting sick. Soon, people started to count the visibly protruding ribs beneath his skin.

"Madam," people would shout at Rebecca, "what happened to this, your big baby? You cannot carry this thing anymore. This is no longer a human being."

Even Azuka's extended family tried to convince him to give them the baby so that they could take him to the witch doctors. But Rebecca refused their offer to take the baby away to die. Dejected but resolute, Rebecca told her husband, "You are not going anywhere with this baby. This is my child, and I cannot throw him away. He is still breathing."

The next morning when Kwemto and Chibuzo were still asleep, she placed Testimony on the bed. Sobbing from angry desperation, she prayed. "God, I did not ask you for another child. You gave him to me. Why should I suffer for this child?"

Gaining strength, she cried out. "God, either you do something about this boy's case, or you take his life. Because from today, henceforth, I will not move an inch, and I am not giving him any medicine from the witch doctor. So, God, if he dies, I say it is you that the shame will go back to.

Falling to her knees, she continued. "This embarrassment is too much for me to bear. God, you just do anything you want with him. But if you do not take his life now, then you must change his situation."

Within a week or so, Testimony started to regain his appetite and then his energy. His cries got louder and his body bigger. "Wow," people said. "This boy will survive it."

"Yes, he will," she said. Everyone but Rebecca was dumbfounded. She knew that God had answered her prayers. At twenty months old, Testimony started to walk—and soon ran energetically.

As Testimony continued to grow, in 2001 Rebecca's husband started to fall ill off and on. The doctors tested Azuka for various illnesses. When Rebecca asked him about his HIV test result, he would not tell her.

"It is positive, huh?" she asked. "Just tell me. I have already cried and cried for HIV and I will not cry again."

"Yes," he said, confirming her suspicions.

With words powerful enough to be spoken quietly, she said, "You see what the lifestyle you have been living has landed you."

Silence.

Finally he said, "But a man's body is not wood; a man cannot stay without a woman for long. It is hard to travel so much and be away from you."

When Rebecca did not validate her husband's defense, he said, "I am sorry. I am so sorry."

"The deed has been done already," she told him in a soft voice. "Just forget it. All you need to do is give your life to Christ and just make your ways right with him. I, for one, have forgiven you. It is for you to forgive yourself now, and ask the Lord also to forgive you."

Azuka hung his head as if he knew that his wife's grace and mercy were unmerited.

She continued. "I do not want to worry. Because if I keep that in my mind, I will keep worrying and I will not be able to help you. You are sick now, and I would not be able to care for you. I would not be able to give you water to drink. It takes forgiveness for me to be able to take care of you the way I am supposed to, sitting close to you on your sickbed and doing all the things I need to do."

From that day on, the two were inseparable.

Two or three days before he died, Azuka told Rebecca, "This room is too bright." She said, "Okay, should I drop the curtains?" She closed them. "No," he said, "it is too bright." Rebecca put out the light. Azuka looked at her and smiled. He said, "You have eyes, but you cannot see. There is a glory in this room. There is a light that you cannot put off. It is shining. I am sorry for you, because you cannot see anything. Your eyes are just there; you cannot see."

Before he died at her side in November of 2001, she told him, "I love you, but God loves you more. Go now."

Rebecca's earlier words were wrong about not having more tears for the tragedies that accompany HIV. Weeping over her husband's death was just a preparation for the coming tsunami of grief.

While their oldest son Kwemto remained healthy and their youngest, Testimony, was growing strong, their middle son Chibuzo began to get sick. He had been born prematurely, and he had been ill with tuberculosis and pneumonia as a toddler. Since then, however, he had grown normally.

"He is grieving the loss of his daddy," people said.

But Chibuzo's health rapidly declined. By August of 2002, Rebecca admitted him to a hospital. A blood test revealed the all-too-familiar three letters: HIV. She was stunned.

Chibuzo's body continued to weaken. Try as he might, he could not fight the virus. Before long, he joined his daddy in heaven.

Rebecca's wails spoke volumes. In her heart, she wrestled with God. "Why would you allow something to happen to him? If I had known sooner that it was HIV, that boy would not have died. I could have done something. I never knew it was HIV. I did not know. It was too late. Oh, God, ohhhhhhhhhhh."

With a protective anger, Rebecca eventually collected herself enough to do what was necessary to nurture her other two sons.

A few months after Chibuzo's death, Rebecca traveled for church business. Her boys stayed with Rebecca's sister, who noticed a rash on Testimony's body. She had heard of the Faith Alive Clinic and took him there. Dr. Chris examined Testimony and suspected the diagnosis.

Before revealing the test result, Dr. Chris asked Testimony's aunt, "Whose child is this?"

"Mine," she said, feeling responsible for her nephew and not thinking much of the question.

He told her gently, "We did a test for your child, and he is positive for HIV. We would like for you to also be tested."

"Now hold on," Rebecca's sister said, "The mother is my junior sister. When she comes back, I will ask her to see you."

When Rebecca returned to Jos, she did not want to go to Faith Alive. But she had to, because Dr. Chris refused to treat Testimony without also treating his mother. Reluctantly, she went. Dr. Chris counseled her about HIV and asked to test her for the virus.

"I already know," she told him.

Dr. Chris looked at her. "What do you know?"

"I know that I have HIV. I have taken the test before."

"Let us still do it again," he said, wanting to confirm the diagnosis before starting mother and child on some type of treatment. Faith Alive did not yet have easy access to lifesaving antiretroviral medications, but did have antibiotics that helped ward off opportunistic infections that prey on weakened immune systems.

"With all pleasure," Rebecca said before taking the test, unconvinced that this doctor had anything to offer.

Because test results at that time took a few days to analyze, Dr. Chris gave her Testimony's medicine and asked her to come back the next week. She did not. "God, I do not feel like going back. If HIV is going to kill me, let me die. I do not want to go to Faith Alive and have everyone looking at me like I am HIV-infected. I do not need anybody else's help. But . . . my son does."

Rebecca steeled her spirit and continued to wrestle with God during the next few months. "If you want me to be a pastor, why did you put HIV in my body? How can I be HIV-infected and still be talking to people about your Word?"

Finally, a thought came to her. "Jesus Christ had to come in the form of human beings. We do not have a high priest that does not feel what we feel."

"So, God, what is the meaning of that? I am not Jesus Christ. I am Rebecca!"

She sensed that God wanted her to know that she needed to go through what she was facing for her to be able to reach out to others. But, like Job, she tried to reason with him. "Ah, God, HIV is not enough? My husband, you took him. My son, you took him. All those things are not enough? Please, I have had enough."

"Yes," she heard a voice in her head say, "it is now time for you to move."

"To where, now?"

"Go to Faith Alive," the voice she heard said. "I want you to strengthen those who are going through what you are going through." She remembered how, in John 9, the disciples asked Jesus about a blind man: "'Rabbi, who sinned, this man or his parents, that he was born blind?'

"'Neither this man nor his parents sinned,' said Jesus, 'but this happened so that the works of God might be displayed in him" (John 9:2b–3).

Finally trusting that God wanted to be glorified in her life, Rebecca went that week to Faith Alive and approached Dr. Chris. "The Lord has asked me to volunteer here," she said boldly, "and I want to go to the counseling unit. I want to reach out to people who are HIV-infected."

Dr. Chris looked at her quizzically. So she showed him her ID card. "Oh, you are a pastor," he said, looking at her with the respect he offered people of God. With a discerning spirit, and not one to stand in the way of God's plan for other people, he introduced her to the head counselor.

In March 2003, Pastor Rebecca began counseling people—eventually numbering in the thousands—before and after their HIV tests. She fearlessly worked with the weekly support group for people with HIV that she was once too ashamed to attend. The sewing and knitting school students began learning from her daily discipleship class lessons, and they looked to her as a role model.

Rebecca started referring pregnant women to Faith Alive's prenatal classes, where nurses teach mothers how to prevent their unborn children from becoming infected with HIV. A simple and inexpensive medicine given at the time of labor and delivery to the mother and to the infant after birth drastically reduces the possibility of HIV infection.

Married couples began coming to Pastor Rebecca to learn that condoms could protect them from catching each other's strains of the virus. And she told women the best way to change their husband's hearts and habits: pray for them in the midst of intimacy.

Back at the "HIV and the Church" training, Pastor Rebecca posed a final question. She had already heard what these pastors and their wives thought about people with HIV. She wanted to talk about the great high priest.

"How do you think Jesus Christ would treat people with HIV if he were here today?" Leaving just a moment for silence, she proceeded to preach about how Jesus ate with the poor, befriended prostitutes, and touched lepers.

"Yes, even lepers," she said. "Jesus touched them. HIV is the modern-day leprosy, and we as the clergy need to lead the way. We need to model for others how to treat people with HIV—in the same loving way that Jesus Christ does—with love, compassion, and forgiveness. Our churches need to be a refuge for suffering people."

"Now," she said, "let us hold the hand of the person sitting next to us and pray." Bowing her head, she started to pray.

"In the mighty name of Jesus. Lord, we ask that you purify our hearts so that we can love others and ourselves unconditionally. Let us not ask people how they got HIV, but how we can help. And let us approach your throne of grace with confidence, so that we may receive mercy and find grace to help us in our time of need. Amen."

Additional Reading

Nossokoff, Erika. *Faith Alive: Stories of Hope and Healing from an African Doctor and His Hospital.* Mustang, OK: Tate, 2012.

11

HIV—Expansion of the Epidemic, Prevention, and Treatment

ARTHUR J. AMMANN

The Beginnings

THE ACQUIRED IMMUNODEFICIENCY SYNDROME (AIDS) was first described in 1981, but its cause remained unknown until 1983, when the human immunodeficiency virus (HIV) was first discovered. The epidemic expanded relentlessly until today it is estimated that there are 31 million people living with HIV/AIDS worldwide, 16 million of whom are women, and 2.5 million of whom are children. New HIV infections continue at a rate of 7,000 each day. In addition, new drugs were discovered that worked by other mechanisms such as preventing attachment of HIV to cells.

Discovery of HIV as the cause of AIDS was an essential step, for, without identifying the precise cause of AIDS, neither a diagnostic test nor treatment could be developed. A diagnostic test for HIV was first approved by the FDA in 1984—a key advance in identifying individuals with the infection, discovering how HIV was spread, and identifying those who might benefit from treatment. The first drug to treat HIV infection, zidovudine, was approved by the FDA in 1987.

HIV was found to be a retrovirus, which meant, to many, that treatment with drugs would be difficult if not impossible. Retroviruses are RNA viruses that are duplicated inside a host cell using an enzyme called reverse transcriptase to produce DNA from its RNA genome. The new DNA is then incorporated into the host's genome by another enzyme called integrase. Once integration occurs, the virus replicates as part of the host cell's DNA. Billions of viruses are produced every day from infected cells in individuals who have been infected. Because HIV replication utilizes the host cell DNA, it was thought that drugs that could interfere with the multiplication of HIV would be too toxic to normal cells or would interfere with the function of cells that were needed to fight off HIV infection. Fortunately, as drugs that inhibit the growth of HIV were discovered, they were found to be less toxic than originally imagined.

The discovery of HIV also accelerated the development of antibody tests, which could be used to identify individuals who were infected and to study the epidemic worldwide. It quickly became clear that HIV was an entirely preventable infection and that HIV transmission was related to behaviors that might be modified to control the epidemic. In spite of early skepticism, behavior change did occur when individuals were educated on how HIV is transmitted and were told of the risk factors associated with HIV transmission. Recent epidemiologic studies have shown that HIV seroprevalence (i.e., the number of individuals infected in a particular population) has been reduced in many countries, including Uganda, Kenya, Zambia, Zimbabwe, parts of India, China, Brazil, Thailand, and the U.S.

There are three main modes of HIV transmission: 1) sexual contact, 2) blood contact, and 3) mother-to-child transmission during pregnancy and breast-feeding. Within each of these three major categories, there are subsets of transmission that will be discussed.

Sexual Transmission

The most common mode of HIV transmission, accounting for approximately 85% of HIV-infected individuals worldwide, is heterosexual unprotected sex. While the initial epidemic was described as occurring primarily in homosexuals—which still accounts for a major portion of HIV infection in the U.S. and Europe—it quickly became clear that heterosexual transmission was the primary means whereby the epidemic spread throughout the world. HIV can be transmitted during heterosexual or homosexual activity and enters the body through the lining of the vagina, vulva, penis, rectum, or mouth during oral sex.

There are well-defined mechanisms associated with increased risk of HIV infection that account for the variations in percentages of individuals infected in different regions of the world. These associations are important to understand in order to tailor public health, educational, and behavioral programs to the needs and practices of the corresponding populations. Not every sexual encounter with someone with HIV results in HIV infection, but there are certain behaviors that contribute to the increased possibility of infection, including having multiple sexual partners, either concomitantly or sequentially. Also contributing to the spread of HIV are certain religious and cultural practices—for instance, wife inheritance, which introduces HIV into a new sexual relationship; sexual cleansing, which involves sexual intercourse between a widow and a relative of her husband after the death of the husband; and marriage practices that involve the marriage of young girls to older men, as many older men are HIV-infected, and young girls are more susceptible to HIV infection.

Per sexual act, HIV is more likely to be acquired through homosexual activity than heterosexual activity. However, women, especially girls and young women, are more susceptible to acquiring HIV from heterosexual activity than men are. This may be a result of a thinner vaginal lining in young girls; the presence of other infections, including other sexually transmitted infections; or physical and sexual abuse.

Understanding how HIV is transmitted sexually is important for intervention programs. One of the most successful HIV-prevention pro-grams was first implemented nationwide in Uganda and was termed the *ABC approach*: "A = abstinence; B = be faithful; C = condoms." Implemen-tation occurred through widespread political and educational campaigns. A significant decrease in new HIV infections in Uganda resulted. With time, however, some of the initial success eroded as behavior reverted back toward more risky sexual activity.

Fundamentally, the "abstinence" approach urged individuals to ab-stain from all sexual activity and encouraged young people to delay their first sexual encounter. The "be faithful" component was understood to mean being faithful to one partner (i.e., a monogamous relationship). This approach required the understanding of lifetime monogamy. Be faithful acknowledged the fact that transmission of HIV could not occur if both sexual partners were HIV-uninfected and remained uninfected.

The "condoms" portion of ABC was controversial among many groups, especially among conservative religious groups who did not believe that condoms should be utilized as a means of birth control or, in the case of HIV, to protect an uninfected sexual partner from HIV. Unfortunately, this meant that HIV could be transmitted from an infected partner, in most instances a male, to an uninfected female partner who was unaware of her partner's HIV status. Under these circumstances, a woman could become HIV-infected "against her will," or without her knowledge. If HIV infection were to occur prior to pregnancy or during pregnancy, HIV could be transmitted to the infant, especially if the mother was unaware of her HIV infection and unable to access treatment to prevent the baby from becoming infected.

Many religious denominations have held fast to the "no condoms in any circumstance" rule without requiring men to be tested for HIV or to abstain from sexual relationships if they are infected—resulting in ongoing HIV transmission. The Roman Catholic Church has recently changed its position on the use of condoms if one sexual partner is HIV-infected and the other is not (discordant couples), stating that it is allowable to use condoms under these circumstances to prevent HIV infection of an uninfected sexual partner.

Early during the implementation of the ABC approach to HIV prevention, there were many skeptics who stated that it was not possible for individuals to change their sexual behavior. However, without knowing precisely if "abstinence," "be faithful," or "condoms" was most effective, it is clear that the rate of HIV infection has decreased in many countries. In the U.S., the number of new HIV infections has decreased from a maximum of 120,000 in 1985 to approximately 55,000 new cases each year. Worldwide, the HIV epidemic declined by 17% between 2001 and 2009.

Contact Tracing

An underutilized approach to preventing HIV transmission is that of contact tracing, also called *partner notification*. There is a long history of controlling sexually transmitted infections through contact tracing. For example, syphilis, gonorrhea, and chlamydia are all sexually transmitted infections, and in the past, when these infections were diagnosed, the affected person's sexual partner was traced and contacted to determine whether they were infected. If so, they were given treatment. If they were not infected, they were counseled on how to protect themselves. This method was especially effective in controlling syphilis. The resistance to performing contact tracing for HIV is derived from the initial history of the HIV epidemic: Because of the association of HIV with homosexuality, in many instances, severe discrimination and stigmatization occurred whenever an individual was identified as HIV-infected. Early in the epidemic there was no treatment for HIV infection, and so it was argued that contact tracing, which often resulted in discrimination, was unnecessary. However, as the epidemic continues to expand—especially to women who lack social, political, and legal power to protect themselves—it would seem that contact tracing should be instituted at this time. The current availability of highly effective lifesaving treatment also argues that individuals with HIV should be contacted early in their disease to maximally benefit from treatment. There continues to be opposition to contact tracing, especially over the concern that if a woman were to reveal her HIV infection status, she would become the object of physical and sexual abuse. However, recent studies indicate that women who live in a situation of ongoing intimate partner violence are more likely to be HIV-infected, and therefore HIV should be considered yet another manifestation of intimate partner violence.

Blood Transfusion and Organ Transplantation

The transmission of HIV results from the transfusion of either untested or inaccurately tested blood products, including red blood cells, platelets, immunoglobulin, and plasma. Blood transmission of AIDS was first documented in 1982. Transfusion of blood products contaminated with HIV used to result in one of the highest rates of HIV transmission, as large amounts of virus were injected directly into the individual. Today, because of blood screening and heat treatment, the risk of getting HIV from blood products is extremely small. Blood banks and blood-collecting centers are required to perform detailed HIV testing utilizing antibody methods as well as highly sensitive PCR methods, which can detect HIV in the blood before antibodies appear—the so-called "window period." In some developing countries, especially those with a high percentage of individuals infected with HIV and without adequate blood-testing methodology, HIV transmission through blood transfusion still occurs. It is estimated that 80,000 to 150,000 HIV infections occur as a result of untested blood donors in resource-poor countries.

Transmission of HIV from organ transplantation has also been documented. All donor material and donors in the U.S. must be tested for HIV before transplantation.

Accidental Inoculation of Infected Blood

Accidental inoculation occurs when a health care worker, nurse, or doctor caring for an individual who has HIV accidentally inoculates themselves with HIV through a needle stick or a significant splash of blood onto an exposed mucous membrane, such as the eye. These are rare occurrences but are nevertheless of concern, in view of the fact that, once infected with HIV, lifelong treatment is required. Administration of postexposure prophylaxis (drugs to prevent infection) can prevent HIV infection from occurring. To be successful, two or more antiretroviral drugs must be administered within 72 hours of the accident and treatment continued for four weeks.

Intravenous Drug Abuse

An additional means of preventing the spread of HIV is that of supplying clean needles and syringes to intravenous drug users. Reuse of needles and syringes, contaminated with blood that often contains HIV and other infectious agents such as hepatitis C and hepatitis B, is a major source of HIV transmission in this population. The provision of clean needles and syringes has been documented to reduce the rate of HIV infection—an inexpensive means of preventing a disease with complications requiring intensive medical care and hospitalizations. Objections to providing clean needles and syringes have come from both religious and nonreligious groups suggesting that this practice may increase the use of illegal drugs and drug addiction. However, deliberately not using a known, effective means of HIV prevention is viewed by many as a punitive approach to a difficult problem that complicates the treatment of drug addiction by adding chronic, debilitating, and often fatal infections to an already difficult situation.

Rape and Sexual Violence

Postexposure prophylaxis (PEP) using antiretroviral drugs is also effective as a means of preventing HIV infection in women who are raped. PEP needs to be administered within 72 hours of rape in order to be effective. The addition of specific antibiotics can also prevent other sexually transmitted infections. High rates of violent rape of girls and women, and often boys and men, occur in politically unstable regions of the world where rule of law does not exist and where rape is often used as a weapon of warfare. Postexposure prophylaxis should also be made available in any context where rape occurs—whether in conflicted regions or in other situations where forcible sex is used on an individual, when the HIV infection status of the perpetrator is unknown. In the U.S. over the last two years, more than 787,000 women were victims of rape or sexual assault.

Mother-to-Child HIV Transmission

Women can transmit HIV to their babies during pregnancy, at birth, or during breast-feeding (perinatal HIV transmission). Approximately one quarter to one third of untreated pregnant women infected with HIV will pass the infection to their babies. If the infant is uninfected after birth, it is possible for the baby to become infected through transmission of the virus from breast milk to the infant's gastrointestinal tract. In 1994, it was shown that the antiretroviral drug zidovudine, given to non–breast-feeding mothers and their infants, reduced HIV transmission to babies by 60%. Today, treatment of pregnant women with highly active antiretroviral therapy (HAART) consisting of three or more drugs can reduce HIV transmission to less than 2%. Recent studies have demonstrated that the use of HAART alone, even if mothers continue to breast-feed, can result in less than 2% transmission to the infants.

HIV infection of newborns has been almost eradicated in the United States as a result of early diagnosis and treatment of mothers who have HIV with HAART. In the U.S., there are fewer than 100 infants born infected each year as a result of treatment. Prevention of mother-to-child HIV transmission in resource-poor countries has been marginally successful. In spite of our knowledge of how to prevent HIV infection of infants since 1994, it is estimated that less than 20% of pregnant women with HIV in resource-poor countries receive any antiretroviral therapy. This accounts for an ongoing 450,000 HIV-infected infants born each year in resource-poor countries. Not all infants born to HIV-infected mothers become infected, but even those infants who undergo treatment or who remain uninfected may eventually become orphans as a result of the death of their HIV infected mothers—a number estimated at some 5 to 6 million each year.

Circumcision

There is a long medical history of the relationship between circumcision and the transmission of disease. Observations dating back to the 19th century suggested that circumcision reduced cervical cancer in women. These studies were performed on Jewish women where a high rate of male circumcision existed. Another study found a low rate of cervical cancer in nuns, suggesting that sexual abstinence also resulted in a reduced incidence of cervical cancer. The association of circumcision with a reduced incidence of cervical cancer suggested that circumcision reduced transmission of the human papilloma virus (HPV), a cause of cervical cancer. More recently, studies performed in Africa demonstrate that male circumcision reduces HIV infection by 60%. Unfortunately, for reasons that are not clear, the protective effect of circumcision did not provide any protection for women.

Other Considerations

There is no evidence that HIV is spread by contact with saliva, sweat, tears, urine, or feces. The lining of the mouth, however, can be infected by HIV, and instances of HIV transmission through oral sex have been reported. Studies of caregivers and families of HIV-infected people have shown that HIV is not spread through casual contact, sharing of food, utensils, towels, bedding, swimming pools, telephones, toilet seats, shaking hands, or hugging. HIV is not spread by biting insects such as mosquitoes or bedbugs.

Pre-Exposure Prophylaxis

Pre-Exposure Prophylaxis (PrEP) refers to the administration of antiretroviral drugs to individuals not infected by HIV to prevent HIV infection when they have sexual intercourse with an individual who has HIV—in contrast to Post-Exposure Prophylaxis, which provides antiretroviral drugs after accidental inoculation or rape. Recent clinical trials in which sexual partners infected with HIV engaged in high-risk sexual intercourse with sexual partners uninfected by HIV who were taking daily antiretroviral drugs (PrEP) showed a 60% reduction in HIV infection of the uninfected partners. To date, PrEP has only been shown to be effective in men who have sex with men (MSM) and in transgendered women who have sex with men; PrEP has not been shown to protect heterosexual women previously uninfected with HIV. There remain significant economic and ethical questions related to the high cost of daily antiretroviral treatment versus the use of less expensive and more readily available prevention methods, such as condoms, reduction in sexual partners, and abstinence.

Diagnosis of HIV Infection

HIV is diagnosed by taking a small amount of blood from a vein or a finger stick and testing it for antibodies to the virus. The timing of HIV testing is important. After HIV infection, there may be only minor symptoms, often flu-like, followed by an asymptomatic period. Usually antibodies do not appear until one to three months after infection, but it may take as long as six months. The PCR test detects HIV in the blood and is often positive as early as two weeks after infection. The most commonly used test to detect HIV is the rapid antibody test, which can provide results in two hours after testing and is less expensive than other antibody tests. Antibodies to HIV can also be detected in saliva and urine. Recently a home-based test for HIV using saliva was approved by the FDA.

Antibody screening of individuals who are at risk for HIV, namely sexually active individuals, is essential for controlling the HIV epidemic. It is estimated that approximately 100,000 individuals in the United States are unaware of their HIV infection. The number worldwide is much greater. This has two consequences. First, treatment of HIV is most effective when started early following infection. If an individual waits until they are symptomatic before being tested for HIV and treatment is started in a more advanced stage of the infection, the antiretroviral drugs may not work well. Second, individuals who are infected but unaware of their infection are more likely to transmit HIV infection to other sexual partners. HIV testing offers an opportunity to counsel individuals on how to prevent HIV transmission and how to protect themselves from HIV if they test negative.

Anyone can be tested anonymously at many sites in the U.S. if they are concerned about confidentiality. Because HIV testing identifies individuals who can be treated with life-saving antiretroviral drugs and individuals who can be counseled as to how to prevent HIV infection, universal offering of HIV testing is recommended. "Universal offering" means that HIV testing is offered in all health care settings regardless of perceived risk for HIV. Individuals maintain the right to refuse testing; however, individuals who test positive for HIV should inform their sexual partners of the test results so that they can protect themselves from HIV infection and, if already infected, benefit from early treatment.

Difficulties arise when using antibody-based HIV testing for babies born to mothers infected with HIV. All babies carry their mothers' antibodies to HIV for several months. Therefore, an antibody test during this time cannot differentiate between the mother's antibodies and the antibodies that may have been produced by the infected baby. The mother's antibodies do not entirely disappear from the baby's bloodstream until 12 months of age. HIV infection in the baby can be diagnosed as early as two weeks after birth if the HIV PCR test, which detects the virus instead of antibodies, is available.

Treatment of HIV Infection

Unfortunately, treatment is not automatically provided following a diagnosis of HIV infection. Treatment guidelines utilized by health organizations were developed by HIV experts following clinical research studies on the effectiveness of treatment in hundreds of thousands of patients throughout the world. Currently, early treatment, before symptoms of HIV develop, is most often recommended as the most effective means of controlling HIV infection and prolonging the life of individuals. Early treatment reduces the complications of HIV—including opportunistic (secondary) infections, cancer, and HIV disease progression. HIV is now considered a chronic disease, and, although there are complications of treatment, most HIV-infected individuals can lead healthy and productive lives for many decades. Once an individual is infected with HIV, even when HAART is provided, there is no evidence that HIV can be cured.

HIV treatment practices in developing countries are significantly different from those in resource-rich countries. Treatment of HIV requires three or more drugs to be given for the lifetime of the individual. In countries with high rates of HIV infection, such as South Africa, Swaziland, and Botswana, the financial and human costs of HIV treatment are extreme: Financial demands, as well as demands on the productivity of health care workers, cause significant stress upon the infrastructure of the health care system. Consequently, treatment guidelines were developed to take into account economic factors such as cost of drugs and duration of treatment even though the recent introduction of generic drugs have reduced the annual cost of HIV treatment of individuals by 50 fold. The use of a dominant economic basis for treatment raises significant ethical issues. Limiting the treatment of individuals with HIV on an economic basis because of the cost of drugs is shortsighted, as untreated individuals with HIV are more likely to develop costly complications of HIV infection, such as opportunistic infections and tuberculosis. In addition, delaying treatment increases the number of required hospitalizations and clinic visits. The premature death of parents from advanced AIDS because of delays in treatment results in a secondary epidemic of orphans, now estimated to be greater than 16 million—far more costly than initially providing the necessary antiretroviral drugs to control HIV infection.

Treatment decisions are usually based on symptoms and on the CD4 lymphocyte count. The CD4 lymphocyte is the primary cell infected with HIV; as the infection progresses, the amount of these cells declines rapidly. A significant reduction in the number of CD4 cells indicates that the virus is not under control and that treatment should be started. A CD4 level of 500 or less is usually an indication for initiating treatment, but there are increasing numbers of expert clinicians that feel the treatment should be started as soon as HIV infection is diagnosed. In 2012 the U.S. Public Health Service recommended initiating treatment in all HIV infected individuals regardless of CD4 count.

In contrast to the controversy about starting treatment at a specific CD4 level, there is universal agreement that treatment should be initiated immediately in patients who are symptomatic. Symptoms include weight loss; unexplained, persistent fevers or recurrent infections; fungal infections of the mouth or vagina; swollen lymph nodes; night sweats; and opportunistic infections (i.e., infections that do not occur in individuals with normal immune systems). The term *AIDS* applies to the most advanced stages of HIV infection. In people with AIDS, these infections are often severe and sometimes fatal because the immune system is so ravaged by HIV that the body cannot fight off certain bacteria, viruses, fungi, and parasites.

Once a decision has been made to initiate treatment for HIV, three or more drugs are utilized. They must be given on a daily basis. The use of a single drug, or discontinuing the use of the drugs, predisposes the individual to developing a virus that is resistant to treatment. HIV is a virus that multiplies rapidly: More than 1 billion viruses are produced each day, contributing to the potential for drug-resistant mutations and thus complicating the long-term treatment of HIV.

Drugs Used for Treatment

The first drug ever approved for the treatment of HIV was zidovudine—approved in 1987. The Food and Drug Administration (FDA) has since approved more than 30 drugs and combination of drugs for treating HIV infection. The first group of drugs used to treat HIV infection, called *nucleoside reverse transcriptase inhibitors (NRTI)*, interrupts an early stage of the virus, preventing HIV from making copies of itself. These drugs may slow the spread of HIV in the body and delay the start of opportunistic infections. This class of drugs, called *nucleoside analogs*, include, for example, zidovudine, lamivudine, stavudine, and tenofovir.

The second class of drugs to be developed are called *non-nucleoside reverse transcriptase inhibitors (NNRTIs)*—for example, nevirapine and efavirenz. Like NRTIs they interrupt virus repletion at an early stage of replication.

The FDA has approved a third class of drugs for treating HIV infection. These drugs, called *protease inhibitors*, interrupt the virus from making copies of itself at a later step in its life cycle. They include, for example, ritonavir, viracept, and nelfinavir.

The FDA also has approved a fourth class of drugs, known as fusion inhibitors, to treat HIV infection. Fuzeon (enfuvirtide; T-20), the first approved fusion inhibitor, works by interfering with HIV-1's ability to enter into cells by blocking the merging of the virus with the cell membranes. This inhibition blocks HIV's ability to enter and infect the human immune cells. Fuzeon is designed for use in combination with other anti-HIV treatments. It reduces the level of HIV infection in the blood and may be active against HIV that has become resistant to current antiviral treatment schedules.

Two additional classes of drugs have been approved by the FDA. Selzentry (maraviroc) is an entry inhibitor that blocks receptors on cells known as CCR5. Isentress (raltegravir) is an integrase inhibitor.

Because HIV can become resistant to any of these drugs, health care providers must use a combination treatment to effectively suppress the virus. When multiple drugs (three or more) are used in combination, it is referred to as *highly active antiretroviral therapy*, or *HAART*, (also referred to as simply *combination antiretroviral therapy* or *(ART)* and can be used by people who are newly infected with HIV as well as by people with AIDS.

Researchers have credited HAART as being a major factor in significantly slowing the progression of HIV infection to AIDS and reducing the number of deaths from AIDS. While HAART is not a cure for AIDS, it has greatly improved the health of many people with AIDS, and it reduces the amount of virus circulating in the blood to nearly undetectable levels. Researchers, however, have shown that HIV remains present in hiding places, such as the lymph nodes, brain, testes, and retina of the eye—even in people who have been treated.

Treatment as Prevention

Treatment with HAART has been so effective in reducing the amount of virus in an individual that the concept of treatment as prevention has been promoted. For several decades it was well known that reducing the amount of virus in the blood of a pregnant woman with HIV reduced the possibility of HIV transmission to her infant. Much larger clinical research studies were required to demonstrate that reducing the amount of virus in the blood of those with HIV also reduced HIV transmission to sexual partners. It is not surprising, therefore, that there is now a correlation with HAART treatment of adults with HIV and decreased transmission through sexual intercourse. While the full impact of HAART treatment on the global HIV epidemic has not been defined, it is anticipated that, as more individuals receive HAART to treat their HIV infection, there will be a significant reduction of HIV infection in sexual partners—impacting the HIV epidemic worldwide.

Conclusions

HIV is a preventable infection. Education and public health approaches have reduced the number of newly infected individuals throughout the world, providing encouragement that the HIV epidemic can be brought under control. For individuals who are already infected, the initiation of early treatment has prolonged their lives, reduced the complications of HIV—including the requirement for multiple clinic visits and hospitalizations—and has allowed individuals to return to productive and useful lives. Education, scientific advances, and political action will help to control the HIV epidemic, but individual behavior change is an absolute necessity to take advantage of prevention methods and treatment. Even with significant reductions in the cost of HAART, from over $6000 per year to less than $120 per year, the economic and human toll of the epidemic continues. The yearly estimated number of 3 million new infections worldwide remains of great concern as HIV infection continues to destroy individuals, families, and communities. Women continue to be more susceptible to HIV infection as a consequence of their inferior social, political, and economic status which prevents them from protecting themselves from unwanted HIV infection. Those who are uninfected are deserving of the dignity and protection afforded to women by sound theological principles. Those who are already infected are deserving of finding a refuge within a Christian community that provides physical, psychosocial and spiritual support that is devoid of stigma and discrimination.

Additional Reading

Centers for Disease Control (CDC). Online: http://www.cdc.gov

Global Strategies for HIV Prevention. Online: http://www.globalstrategies.org

HIV InSite. Online: http://hivinsite.ucsf.edu

National Institutes of Health (NIAID). Online: http://www.niaid.nih.gov

UNAIDS. Online: http://www.unaids.org

Whiteside, Alan. *HIV/AIDS: A Very Short Introduction*. Oxford: Oxford University Press, 2008.

Women, Children, and HIV. Online: http://www.womenchildrenhiv.org

12

The Church as a Refuge
for Women Affected by HIV

NUPANGA WEANZANA

THE SIZE OF THE HIV epidemic and the number of individuals that it has affected dwarfs any infectious disease epidemic recorded in history. Nowhere is this situation more urgent than on the continent of Africa, and in particular in Sub-Saharan Africa where more than 65% of the people who have HIV live. Clearly, theological principles from both the Old and New Testaments concerning the dignity of women within the HIV epidemic apply universally to all women who seek refuge from pain and suffering through a spiritual community that lives out the teachings of Jesus. The Christian Church everywhere needs to become fully engaged in the HIV epidemic. Women and children bear the greater burden of the HIV epidemic. Women are more easily infected; they are unable to refuse sexual intercourse with a man, even if he is HIV-infected; they suffer the guilt of transmitting HIV to their infants in utero or when breast-feeding; they are discriminated against, even if they are infected by men; and they have diminished access to treatment and care. Economically, culturally, politically, and—tragically—even religiously, women are selectively stigmatized, shunned, blamed, and often refused the refuge offered by the Christian community to others who are suffering. Whether they are infected or not, children of women with HIV are likely to become orphans; are frequently stigmatized or demonized; lose their family and community support; and may lose all rights to their inheritance.

Early on, the response of the Christian Church to the HIV epidemic was muted. That has changed significantly, but is the response of the Christian Church still insufficient to bring comfort and aid to women suffering with HIV?

The Old and New Testaments tell us unambiguously and without qualification that it is our responsibility to care for widows and orphans. The psalmist identifies God as one who is a "father to the fatherless" and a "defender of widows" (Psalm 68:5). Jesus tells the story of the king who separates his followers into those who respond to the needs of the poor and sick and those who do not (Matthew 25:31–46). The book of James states that a religion that is pure and faultless includes caring for widows and orphans (James 1:27). Today, these widows would likely be infected with HIV, as is the case for thousands of prostitutes in our societies. Paradoxically, in spite of these teachings, too much of the discrimination against women emanates from the Christian Church and raises questions as to how the teachings of Jesus are interpreted in relation to women and HIV. In Africa, and indeed in most of the world's countries, the role and place of the women in the Church is often peripheral.

Consider the story of the Samaritan woman whom Jesus met at the well. She was a woman who was on the fringes of society and ostracized by her own people. Everything about her seemed to put distance between her and her community. It was not surprising that she went alone to draw water from a well at midday, when no one else would be there—except, on this one day, there was someone who took a deliberate detour to meet with her there.

The fact that she was of the wrong gender, practiced the wrong religion, lived in the wrong location, and was a prostitute did not deter Jesus from setting the example, early in his ministry, for how he viewed women who were the focus of exclusion and discrimination. Today, this woman would likely be infected with HIV.

Throughout the HIV epidemic, there have been barriers to a compassionate response to those infected by HIV that cannot be justified through biblical principles. They are barriers that could have been bridged with the same love and forgiveness that Jesus showed to the woman at the well, or to the woman caught in adultery who was about to be stoned to death, or the woman who wiped his feet with her tears and was condemned by the religious leaders. It seems as if the vastness of Jesus's teaching on love, compassion, and forgiveness is not sufficiently persuasive to reach out to all those suffering from HIV, especially women.

Women and children—widows and orphans—who now dominate the HIV epidemic, languish with a devastating viral infection that draws recrimination and stigmatization and produces enormous needs. In their suffering, they turn to the Church as a refuge, but too often they are turned away and left wondering, "Where is the love; where is the forgiveness; where is the compassion?" Many in the Christian Church wonder the same and ask, "If we cannot provide a refuge for women who suffer from HIV, then what do the teachings of Jesus mean?"

There are many faith-based organizations and many Christians who reach out to those with HIV and provide for those suffering from HIV; but, considering the magnitude of the epidemic, the response is insufficient. The entire unified body of Christ is needed.

There are too many Christian leaders and followers who have engaged in the selective exclusion of women with HIV from the Christian community, or, worse, have promulgated cultural and theological positions that purportedly justify the exclusion of these women from the body of Christ. The tragic result is to preclude the Church from becoming a refuge for all who suffer.

Because we believe that the Christian Church can—and must—take a leadership role in protecting the millions of women and children who are at risk for HIV infection or who are already infected, we conducted a workshop on HIV, women, and the Church at Bangui Evangelical School of Theology (FATEB) in Central African Republic. The intent of the workshop was to establish a scientifically and theologically sound understanding of the HIV epidemic; to foster an understanding of the necessity of a leadership role for faith-based communities in providing a loving, compassionate, and forgiving response to those who are affected by HIV; and to define the means by which faith-based communities can reflect the character of Jesus Christ in responding to the HIV epidemic.

There were many topics that were discussed during the conference. The two issues that caused unrest were: "Why is the Christian Church not a universal refuge for those who are infected with HIV? Why is the Church so often the source of stigma and discrimination?"

Martin Luther King Jr. once said, "The greatest tragedy of this generation, which history will record, is not the vitriolic words of those who hate, or the aggressive acts of others, but the appalling silence of the good people." For Christians worldwide, the HIV epidemic, especially as it affects women, has been closed in a cloak of silence by the many good people.

At the conclusion of the Bangui conference, a consensus document was drafted with the prayer that the Christian Church would once again be distinguished, as Jesus was, as protector of women and children and a refuge for all who suffer, including women with HIV. The consensus statement that follows was drafted by those who attended the conference in Central African Republic and who participated in the presentations, discussions, and prayers. It is not derived from an American view of what the Christian Church in Africa should do. Rather, it represents a plea from African pastors, seminarians, students, and women with HIV, who suffer the greater burden of the HIV epidemic, for all Christians—whether in Africa, Asia, China, India, South America, the U.S., or Europe—to return the Christian Church to its role as a refuge for all of those who suffer and who seek the reality of the love, compassion, and forgiveness that Jesus taught.

The Bangui Declaration on the Importance of Christian Communities in HIV Prevention, Treatment and Care[1]

As participants in the conference on the Importance of Religious Communities in HIV Prevention, Treatment and Care, held on the campus of the Bangui Evangelical School of Theology, November 17 to 19, 2008, conscious of the role of the Church in the world, in keeping with the mission assigned to it by the Lord, to bear witness to God's love and compassion for humanity, following various presentations on HIV and its effects, and after discussions and debates in targeted workshops, we have adopted the present declaration as a frame of reference to guide our mission and our actions as followers of Jesus in the battle against HIV. We are including this battle against HIV in our mission of proclaiming the uncompromising love and forgiveness of God. The Word of God encourages us to such a commitment as we have been instructed to be the salt of the earth and the light to the world (Matthew 5:13–14) and to overcome evil with good (Romans 12:21). We commit ourselves to this battle against HIV, teaching that prevention at this time remains the only means of avoiding HIV infection and

---

1. Adapted from a conference held at the Bangui Evangelical School of Theology (BEST) Bangui, Central African Republic.

progression to AIDS. The approach we highlight today in HIV prevention is ABC: Abstinence, Be faithful, Condom. (Note some conference participants felt that condoms were a medical product in that the church should not participate in the promotion. However they felt that they should inform their communities that the condom is used as a means of preventing HIV.)

We rejoice in the medical progress that has been made in testing for the HIV virus. We encourage pastors and members of our communities to confirm their HIV status with respect to the virus by making use of the many centers for voluntary testing available in their communities and countries. At the same time, voluntary testing should be accompanied by pastoral or psychological support before and after testing in order to prepare people for possible positive results of their test. We request pastors to encourage young people engaged to be married to determine their status through testing before they are married. Thus, the two persons desiring to be married will enter into their marriage with this knowledge established. If the human and technical means are available, religious communities will create voluntary testing centers. We encourage couples who are married who have engaged in risky sexual behavior that might result in HIV infection to respect the sanctity of their partners and to be tested to protect each other and their children from preventable HIV transmission. The Church must fully engage in its role of providing a place of refuge for those who are in pain and suffering, especially women and children with HIV infection who undergo disproportionate stigmatization and discrimination. Throughout the Old Testament cities of refuge are listed (Numbers 35:6; Deuteronomy 23:15–16). The psalmist and Isaiah speak repeatedly of God as a refuge for those who are afflicted (Isaiah 25:4; Psalm 7:1–2). In light of the rejection and discrimination that often strike people living with HIV, the church remains and shall remain a place of refuge: of compassion, forgiveness and of understanding and love. Following the example of Jesus Christ, who was a refuge for rejected people (John 8:1–11) and who invited all who were weary and heavy-laden to come to Him and receive rest (Matthew 11:28). The church will offer places where people living with HIV will find hope and comfort. As the body of Christ, and as we bear one another's burdens (Galatians 6:2) while we have opportunity, let us do good to all, especially those who are in the household of faith (Galatians 6:10). The Church must create structures for meeting and welcoming people who are accused and rejected, just as Jesus protected the Samaritan woman at the well and the woman taken in adultery from condemnation so that they could recover their physical, moral, spiritual and social dignity (John 4:7–9; 8:3–9). At the same time, the church will not be a substitute for health facilities. The church will direct, as needed, people who are ill to appropriate medical centers. In spite of the lack of a vaccine and the therapeutic means to eradicate HIV, the church will preach the hope that endures even beyond physical death.

In spite of its destructive character, the presence of HIV today in our society represents a fertile field and opportunity for the church to proclaim the message of a holistic salvation in Jesus Christ and to bear witness to the love and infinite grace of God for all humanity. We will grasp this opportunity to translate our love, forgiveness and compassion into action as we follow our Lord Jesus, who accepted every opportunity, good or bad, to proclaim the good news of the Kingdom. The church is called upon to protect women. HIV-infected women today within Central African society and throughout the world constitute an especially vulnerable group. In their dignity and in their intimacy they undergo the terrible consequences of HIV. We will preach and reaffirm that the woman is created in the image of God and that, as such, she shares all the rights of this status (Genesis 1:27). Our words and our actions must contribute to the restoration of the woman's dignity as well as to the defense of her rights in our society. We will fight against every form of violence against women. Also, our teaching and our actions must discourage every form of early or arranged marriages. We affirm that our cultural traditions that disfigure the woman must never replace the message of love and equality in the Gospel (Galatians 3:28). We will also encourage women themselves to resist their own dehumanization. Prostitution and the use of women in advertising the sale of products are acts that steal from women the dignity of a person created in the image of God (1 Timothy 2:9). Promoting the rights of women will lead us to put into place educational processes that will enable women to understand their rights and responsibilities. People living with HIV today are victims of blatant stigmatization in our Central African society as well as other societies. This stigmatization often takes the form of rejection, accusations and the creation of guilt. In his earthly ministry, Jesus involved himself with people who were victims of stigmatization (John 8:3–9). As with the man who was blind from birth, Jesus did not seek to place blame on individuals for their illnesses (John 9:3–5). As places of refuge, our communities will be locations where welcoming and understanding will provide to those experiencing rejection the opportunity for love, compassion, forgiveness and recovering joy and the hope of living. Community leaders and their members must practice a confidentiality that is often missing and leads to discrimination. Stigmatization is also practiced within our communities through the frequent establishment of a connection between the disease and sin. There are diseases that are the result of sin, but not every sickness is the consequence of sin. And even if a disease is due to sin, our communities will not be places of judgment. They will be places of pardon, following the example of Christ, who did not condemn the woman taken in adultery (John 8:1–11). For just as the sufferings of Christ are ours in abundance, so also our comfort is abundant through Christ (2 Corinthians 1:5).

The social dimension of the Gospel asks of us as religious communities to bring our care to people infected and affected by HIV. In our communities we will put into place social structures of assistance and care that will bring relief to these persons. We accept with appreciation the initiative of the Evangelical Association of Churches in the organization of a week of solidarity with those infected and affected by HIV. The care to be offered will avoid creating perpetual dependence by the promotion of revenue-generating activities as an effective means of gaining independence and dignity. Widows and orphans of HIV will find in our communities places of love, understanding and support as we are instructed to provide throughout the Old and New Testaments (Psalm 68:4–6; Isaiah 1:17; James 1:26–2:1). In the care that we will bring to infected persons, we will seek to guide the sick to the treatment, including anti HIV drugs, they require, making them well.

As the Unified Body of Christ, We Seek to Set an Example to Others

Our actions will take various forms:

1. Promotion of the Church as a refuge for those who are infected and affected by HIV.

2. Organization of awareness-raising messages through the media (radio, TV, etc.).

3. Organization of special religious services for awareness-raising and support.

4. Organization of teaching regarding HIV aimed at different ages and groups in our communities.

5. Promotion of prevention against HIV in our main worship and other services.

6. Encouragement of our leaders to be examples in voluntary testing.

7. Open discussion of HIV and the need for love, forgiveness and compassion.

8. Using the reality of HIV to preach the Gospel of God's love to people.

9. Offering special protection to women who are victims of HIV.

10. Defending the rights of widows and orphans.

11. Creating within our communities support groups for infected persons and for the families affected by HIV. This will be spiritual, moral and material support.

12. Organization of periodic meetings to share experiences and to augment the capabilities of leaders.

With honor to God and the teachings of Jesus Christ, we ask the body of Christ to support the actions written above. We ask God to help us and to support us as we put all these things into practice for his glory.

APPENDIX 1

The 20 Most Frequently Asked Questions about HIV and AIDS

1. What is the Human Immunodeficiency Virus?

Human Immunodeficiency Virus, or HIV, was recognized as the cause of AIDS in 1983. It is a retrovirus, a type of virus that inserts its genetic information into the cells of the host and directs the cells to produce large amounts of HIV.

2. Where did HIV come from?

Researchers and scientists believe that HIV came from a particular kind of chimpanzee in Western Africa. As humans hunted animals in the forests, they may have become infected—perhaps through a knife or spear wound. Recent studies indicate that HIV may have jumped from monkeys to humans as early as the late 1800s. As a result of migration from forests to villages, from villages to cities, and then to the world by means of international travel, HIV is thought to have spread throughout the world primarily through heterosexual sexual relations.

3. What is AIDS?

AIDS is the Acquired Immunodeficiency Syndrome. It is the most severe manifestation of infection with HIV. The U.S. Centers for Disease Control and Prevention (CDC), the World Health Organization (WHO), and many national governments list numerous opportunistic infections and cancers that, in the presence of HIV infection, result in an AIDS diagnosis. AIDS can affect the central nervous system, creating neurological problems. AIDS is also defined on the basis of the degree of immunodeficiency in an individual infected with HIV.

4. How does HIV cause AIDS?

HIV causes AIDS by infecting cells of the immune system that are required to prevent and control infections caused by bacteria, viruses, and fungi. As HIV multiplies, it continues to destroy cells of the immune system until AIDS develops.

5. How is HIV transmitted?

There are three main ways that HIV is transmitted: sexual intercourse, exposure to HIV-infected blood, and transmission of HIV from infected mothers to their infants during pregnancy, delivery—and transmission through breast milk. HIV is not transmitted by casual contact.

6. What are antiretroviral drugs?

Antiretroviral ("against retrovirus") drugs were first approved in 1987. The drugs work by inhibiting enzymes that are required by HIV to multiply. Some drugs prevent attachment of the virus to the cell. There are five major classes of drugs, each of which work by different mechanisms. Treatment of patients who have HIV works best when combinations of drugs are used. The more potent the combination, the more likely virus levels will be reduced and immunity restored, resulting in improved health and reduced numbers of opportunistic infections.

7. Has anyone been cured of HIV?

As far as we know, no one has ever been cured of HIV infection. The virus may remain dormant for many years without producing any symptoms. The conditions that cause AIDS, on the other hand, may be reversible with the use of potent combination antiretroviral therapy.

8. How do antiretroviral drugs work to prevent HIV infection of infants?

Studies in pregnant women who have HIV demonstrate that drugs such as nevirapine and combination drugs, often called highly active antiretroviral therapy (HAART), prevent HIV infection of the infant by two mechanisms. First, they lower the amount of virus in the mother, thereby reducing the possibility of transmitting the virus to the infant. Second, they provide "post-exposure prophylaxis," whereby the drug prevents the infant's cells from becoming infected. HAART, given to the mother throughout pregnancy and during breast-feeding, is more effective in preventing infection of the infant than single-dose nevirapine.

9. How much HIV transmission to infants can be prevented?

Transmission of HIV is reduced by more than 98% in developed countries using a combination of antiretroviral drugs (reducing viral levels in the mother), Cesarean section (lowering HIV exposure that would otherwise occur during vaginal delivery), and formula feeding of the infant (reducing HIV transmission through breast milk). Getting HAART to treat pregnant women infected with HIV in resource-poor countries is a priority for maximizing the protection of infants exposed to maternal HIV.

10. Why is it necessary to continue breast-feeding if it is a significant source of HIV infection?

Cost of formula and the lack of clean water combine to make formula-feeding difficult. Formula-feeding in developing countries is often associated with increased rates of other infections, diarrhea, and a high infant mortality. Further, mothers who formula-feed are often assumed to be HIV-infected and may suffer discrimination. Currently, exclusive breast-feeding (nothing by mouth except breast milk for 6 months) is recommended as the safest approach to feeding infants in resource-poor settings. New studies demonstrate that protection from HIV transmitted by breast-feeding can be reduced to 2%, comparable to what is seen in the U.S. and in European populations, if antiretroviral treatment for the mother is continued until breast-feeding is stopped.

11. If breast-feeding is known to transmit HIV infection, isn't the protection of HAART lost with continued breast-feeding?

HIV transmission through breast-feeding most likely occurs during the first several months of life. If the level of virus is reduced in breast milk, it is less likely to transmit HIV. Thus, the use of HAART during breast-feeding is essential to dramatically reduce the possibility of HIV transmission to infants.

12. Why do faith-based and non-government organizations require funding if billions of dollars from international organizations are directed to HIV/AIDS in developing countries?

The World Health Organization and the U.S. Congressional/Presidential budget for HIV/AIDS (PEPFAR) account for billions of dollars of assistance each year. The funds are divided between prevention, treatment, and orphan care. The funds also are directed toward tuberculosis and malaria. Although a significant sum of money is allotted, it is estimated that three times the amount is needed just to meet all of the treatment needs. Fewer than 20% of individuals with HIV will receive treatment. The U.S. funds are restricted to 17 countries; all except two are in Africa. This contrasts with the over 165 countries that have reported HIV. As with other donation programs, most resource-poor hospitals and clinics will not be able to access the funds. If a country is not on the list of targeted countries, they will not receive any of the U.S. funds.

13. How much would it cost to treat all of the pregnant women in the world who have HIV with highly active antiretroviral treatment (HAART) for one year?

There are approximately two million pregnant women worldwide infected with HIV, and they give birth yearly to 450,000 infants with HIV. The cost of antiretroviral drugs for these two million women and their infants is less than $500 million per year. However, many countries lack a health care infrastructure adequate for counseling and HIV rapid testing. Nevertheless, getting HAART to pregnant women infected with HIV is absolutely necessary if infant lives are to be saved. Continuing treatment of women with HIV—not just to prevent HIV infection of infants—would keep mothers alive and healthy, prevent orphanhood, and save hundreds of millions of dollars in unnecessary expenses for hospital care and support of orphans.

14. How many lives could be saved each year if HAART were available to treat all pregnant women who have HIV and their infants?

HAART could prevent 95% of HIV infections in 450,000 infants each year. Thus, 427,500 lives could be saved each year—over 4.2 million lives in a decade.

15. How many pregnant women are tested for HIV worldwide, and how many of those who are infected get HAART?

Tragically, less than 20% of pregnant women who have HIV get any treatment to prevent the infection of their infants. This is a result of limited access to HAART and HIV testing, inadequate health care infrastructure, inadequate resources, and unnecessary bureaucratic obstacles that prevent widespread distribution of HAART and training of health care workers.

16. Why do some organizations focus on prevention of HIV transmission from mothers to infants?

Prevention of HIV transmission from mothers to infants is the megaphone that calls attention to the global HIV/AIDS epidemic. Most individuals easily understand it. The cost of establishing programs for HIV prevention, counseling, and testing is much lower than that of treatment programs. Treatment of HIV infection is critical, but, without better prevention, we will never be able to catch up on treatment. For every 100 individuals put on treatment, 250 new infections occur. Individuals, communities, and organizations are receptive to programs that prevent the HIV infection of infants.

17. Is prevention more important than treatment?

Without improved prevention levels, the two to three million new HIV infections each year will continue indefinitely, adding an enormous additional burden to health care costs and human suffering. We must prevent HIV to control the epidemic and to curtail the devastating and ongoing impacts on individuals, families, and communities, as well as the health care burden on an already-stressed health care infrastructure. There is no vaccine to prevent HIV infection on the horizon. But, as is the case for all diseases, when prevention fails, we must provide compassionate treatment and care for those who are infected and help them return to healthy and productive lives.

18. Does treatment do anything toward preventing HIV transmission?

Recent studies indicate that when HIV-infected individuals are treated, they are less likely to transmit HIV infection to a sexual partner when having unprotected sex. This has encouraged the public health community and led to statements that increasing treatment will also prevent expansion of the HIV epidemic. The reduction in transmission of HIV by an individual who is undergoing treatment is not 100%, however, and it is still possible that an uninfected sexual partner will become infected if precautions are not taken (e.g., practicing abstinence, reducing the number of sexual partners, using condoms).

19. Can we be optimistic?

We see individuals and organizations around the world implementing programs for the prevention of HIV transmission from mothers to infants—many of them with limited resources. The downturn in the global economy has slowed the implementation of prevention and care programs but in spite of these issues much progress has been made. Worldwide, we are beginning to see HIV prevention have an effect. The number of new HIV infections has decreased in the U.S., Uganda, Kenya, Zambia, Zimbabwe, Thailand, China, Brazil, and India, and many other countries have seen a stabilization of the number of new infections. Nevertheless, HIV prevention must continue as a priority.

20. What can we do?

Donate: Choose the organization carefully. Be certain that prevention and treatment reach the maximum number of people. Look for accountability and low overhead.

Write: Keep pressure on the U.S. Congress and the President. HIV disrupts families and communities, and it destabilizes governments. This is not justice and equity in health care.

Advocate: Women and children require special protection. Most often, they do not benefit as much as men do from HIV prevention and treatment programs. Discrimination, stigmatization, sexual violence, and an inability to control sexual choices, especially in girls and young women, continue to drive the disproportionate number of infections in women and children.

Educate: Learn the sound scientific facts and principles about HIV and AIDS. Talk to those you know about how you can respond to an individual with HIV to prevent stigmatization and discrimination—especially against women and children who are HIV-infected. Discuss, teach, and present wherever you can that communities and faith-based organizations must be a refuge for those who are in pain and suffering and who have no place to turn for help.

APPENDIX 2

Christian Organizational and Denominational Statements on HIV and AIDS[1]

Compiled and edited by

ARTHUR J. AMMANN

Introduction

MANY FAITH-BASED ORGANIZATIONS AND denominations have developed documents for a Christian-based approach to the issues precipitated by the HIV epidemic. This chapter includes selected statements from denominations, organizations, universities, and colleges that reflect their theological views. This is not meant to be an exhaustive compilation of available documents. Rather, the purpose is to provide several well-reasoned Christian responses. The thread running through these documents has its foundations in the teaching of Jesus and the historical response of Christians to epidemics and calamities throughout the centuries. They share in a clear call for Christians to avoid discrimination and condemnation and respond to those who suffer—regardless of cause—with forgiveness, love, compassion, and care as taught by Jesus.

The statements provided below are not necessarily the entire statement but may be abbreviated to accommodate the length of the appendix while maintaining respect for the author's objectives. In a few instances, where new information is available and where the statements have not been updated, contradictory statements have been deleted. Minor edits, which

---

1. Published with the permission of the organizations and denominations represented.

did not change the intent of the statements, were made to enhance readability. All statements have been used with permission. Internet addresses have been provided for the reader who desires to refer to the original statement or to obtain additional information or clarification.

International Christian Medical & Dental Association Merroo Statement[2]

The statement grew out of the International Christian Medical and Dental Association (ICMDA) International AIDS Pre-conference at Merroo, New South Wales, in July 2006.

Summary

We are motivated by a belief in a loving God who cares about all the world's people regardless of health status, race, creed, color, or financial or social standing. We continue to encourage all Christian health workers, services, institutions, local congregations, and communities to engage holistically in HIV and AIDS advocacy, education, prevention, care, and treatment. We support the call for universal access to prevention and treatment as part of a right to health and dignity for all.

Situation

We the member bodies of the International Christian Medical & Dental Association (ICMDA) note with concern the severity of the HIV and AIDS epidemic throughout the world and the inadequate resources allocated to fight it. Furthermore, we note with sadness the continued impact of the epidemic especially in vulnerable populations, including women and girls, the poor, commercial sex workers, intravenous drug users, and men who have sex with men.

Commendation

We take note of and commend the efforts currently being made by many governments, non-government organizations, faith-based organizations,

2. Online: http://www.icmdahivinitiative.org/pages/merroo-statement.php.

and churches, in a multi-sectoral collaborative approach within the framework of national and international strategies. We recognize with appreciation the work in HIV and AIDS already being done by the medical and dental workers of the many national Christian Medical and Dental Fellowships and their members. We welcome the many innovative responses and the leadership of Christians in addressing HIV and AIDS.

Challenge

We commit ourselves to building capacity and taking appropriate action to respond to the epidemic. We must address gender, cultural, social, and economic practices as well as the poverty that increases the impact of HIV and AIDS in our societies. We recognize the challenge to our churches and professions to engage their societies to address stigma, widow and orphan care, and social and economic support for people living with HIV and AIDS.

Call to Action

We continue to encourage all Christian health workers, services, institutions, local congregations, and communities to engage holistically in HIV and AIDS advocacy, education, prevention, care, and treatment. We support the call for universal access to prevention and treatment as part of a right to health and dignity for all. We advocate for the rights of vulnerable groups such as women, children, youth, and people living with HIV and AIDS. We will create an enabling environment and seek to work alongside these groups.

As members of the ICMDA, we will develop, strengthen, and apply our medical and dental knowledge, skills, and resources within a theology of health, justice, and dignity. We commit to reduce stigma, discrimination, denial, and silence. We commit to review our actions in response to this declaration at future ICMDA International and regional congresses. Our call to action is with a humble, repentant, and prophetic spirit, learning with those who are already engaged. Scientific knowledge and good professional practice, together with prayer, networking, and partnership, will be central in our response to HIV and AIDS. Because all people are created in the image of God, we will demonstrate Christian love to the infected and affected, and affirm the dignity and human rights of all.

The Adventist Development and Relief Agency (ADRA): Statement on AIDS[3]

Acquired immunodeficiency syndrome (AIDS) and associated conditions are spreading rapidly around the world. On the basis of statistical studies it is estimated that in the near future, in many countries of the world, every church congregation numbering 100 or more will include at least one member who has a friend or relative with AIDS.

AIDS is transmitted through two major sources: sexual intimacy with an infected person, and introduction of HIV (human immunodeficiency virus) contaminated blood into the body either through injections with unsterile needles and syringes or through contaminated blood products. AIDS can be prevented by avoiding sexual contact before marriage and maintaining a faithful monogamous relationship with an uninfected person in marriage, and by avoiding the use of unsterile needles for injections and assuring the safety of blood products.

Adventists are committed to education for prevention of AIDS. For many years Adventists have fought against the circulation, sale, and use of drugs, and continue to do so. Adventist support sex education that includes the concept that human sexuality is God's gift to humanity. Biblical sexuality clearly limits sexual relationships to one's spouse and excludes promiscuous and all other sexual relationships and the consequent increased exposure to HIV.

The Christlike response to AIDS must be personal—compassionate, helpful, and redemptive. Just as Jesus cared about those with leprosy, the feared communicable disease of His day, His followers today will care for those with AIDS. James advised, "What good is there in your saying to them, 'God bless you! Keep warm and eat well!'—if you don't give them the necessities of life?" (James 2:16, TEV).

3. Online: http://www.adra.org/site/PageNavigator/work/special/the_hiv_and_aids _crisis/aids_response.

HIV/AIDS and Wheaton College April, 2007[4]

The global HIV/AIDS pandemic is one of the greatest humanitarian crises of our day. Although in the West HIV/AIDS is a chronic disease that has become increasingly treatable with proper medical care, among the poor of the global south it is often fatal. AIDS tends to cluster in families, killing adults and leaving their children orphaned and sick. Because proper nutrition and access to health care remain beyond the reach of most people in the global south, this renders the diagnosis of an HIV infection an imminent death sentence.

The suffering and death resulting from HIV/AIDS stands in stark contrast to God's intentions for abundant life. This unprecedented pandemic thus confronts the world with a complex crisis of profound proportions, including medical, scientific, logistical and structural challenges. It also raises for Christ's church a series of theological and moral challenges.

How are we to respond to such challenges? The following represents our commitment to reflect faithfully upon our Christian responsibilities in the face of this global threat. We acknowledge our responsibility to proclaim the Gospel of Jesus Christ and embody his commands for justice, sexual purity, forgiveness, and compassionate action for those who suffer.

A Biblical Response

Christ and the Promise of Life

Scripture repeatedly reminds us that God animates, sustains, and protects life (John 1:4; Amos 5:4; cf. Ezekiel 18:32). Thus our theological reflection on the HIV/AIDS pandemic must be grounded in a theology of life. God's gifts of life, dignity and love obligate humans to glorify him in faithful obedience. These gifts extend to all humanity, the just and the unjust, because God's redemptive love encompasses the world.

A truly Christian theology of life will be, moreover, thoroughly Christ-centered. He who created life (John 1:3–4) also joined the human race, giving himself to die in order that we may live. Jesus has entered into the suffering and brokenness of the world and won victory over death through his own suffering and weakness.

The HIV/AIDS pandemic thus calls for a consistent Christ-centered theology of life, one in which human existence is properly understood as

4. Online: http://www.wheaton.edu/.

life before the living God. The devastating threat posed by HIV/AIDS challenges us both to affirm the life and dignity which flow from God's creative and sacrificial love, and to do all we all we can to enhance them.

Compassion and Justice

With the framers of the first Lausanne Covenant (1974) we express "penitence both for our neglect and for having sometimes regarded evangelism and social concern as mutually exclusive. Although reconciliation with other people is not reconciliation with God, nor is social action evangelism, nor is political liberation salvation, nevertheless we affirm that evangelism and socio-political involvement are both part of our Christian duty" (Article 5, "Christian Social Responsibility").

God calls his people "to act justly and to love mercy and to walk humbly with your God" (Micah 6:8). He honors those who stop to care for suffering strangers (Luke 10:29–37). Thus the Apostle Paul instructs us, "Let us not become weary in doing good. As we have opportunity, let us do good to all people, especially to those who belong to the family of believers" (Galatians 6:9–10).

Jesus summarizes the entire law when he commands us to "'Love the Lord your God with all your heart and with all your soul and with all your strength and with all your mind,' and 'Love your neighbor as yourself'" (Luke 10:25–28). Just as the church responds to the needs of the unborn, the homeless, and the persecuted church, so also the love of Christ compels us (2 Corinthians 5:14–15) to offer ourselves in sacrificial service to those who suffer, especially to the most vulnerable and fragile of our neighbors (James 1:27).

According to the Bible, justice and mercy are inseparable (Isaiah 11:1–5; Psalm 113:5–9). Thus, in addition to caring for those who suffer (acts of mercy), we are also called to proclaim a holistic Gospel. Not only must we speak truthfully about individual sin such as sexual promiscuity and drug use; we must also by extension speak truthfully about ineffective political and economic structures, poverty, and inadequate health care, and about institutionalized sin such as government corruption, organized crime, and economic oppression, all of which contribute to the spread of HIV.

Sexual Fidelity and Obedience

The watershed All Africa Church and AIDS Consultation (1994) declared that, "HIV/AIDS is inextricably intertwined with human sexuality. Through the indiscriminate practice of sex outside of marriage, HIV is taking advantage of one of the most beautiful God-gifted expressions of love that can be shared by two people. The church's unique biblical perspective can serve to both preserve the loving expression of human sexuality intended by God and protect human relationships from the destructive and divisive nature of HIV."

This statement is based upon the assumption that human disease, suffering and death ultimately result from Adam and Eve's sin and God's subsequent curse. The HIV/AIDS pandemic in particular has been driven largely by sexual relations outside of marriage, and by complex social and political forces. We believe that God has commanded sexual fidelity in marriage and sexual abstinence outside of marriage. Thus, we believe that prevention of HIV/AIDS begins by calling all to a life of sexual purity. We also believe, however, that Scripture warns against the conclusion that suffering and disease can be easily correlated with sin (see Job, John 9:1–3; Luke 13:1–5). A Christian response to this crisis must therefore resist simplistic claims about HIV/AIDS and divine judgment.

Our Response

HIV/AIDS confronts us with the call to serve with compassion and mercy in the midst of a profound human crisis. By God's grace, we must not "pass by on the other side" (Luke 10:31).

The College's mission as a Christian institution of higher learning dedicated to the development of whole and effective Christians carries with it an obligation to respond in appropriate ways to the pandemic of HIV/AIDS. As a Christian learning community made up of faculty, staff, students, and alumni, we seek to carry out the mission of the College by demonstrating faithful and informed reflection upon this crisis. In addition, we acknowledge our responsibility to proclaim the Gospel of Jesus Christ and embody his commands for justice, sexual purity, forgiveness, and compassionate action for those who suffer.

In the fulfillment of this obligation, we aim to foster student involvement in addressing the pandemic. In addition, we seek to encourage our faculty to teach effectively about HIV/AIDS across the disciplines, and to develop staff engagement through further education and opportunity. We affirm Wheaton's global alumni who have made significant contributions and we seek to encourage them as they continue to respond through health care, education, government, non-government organizations, and grassroots support groups. Even as we seek to equip future graduates, the College recognizes the value of listening to our alumni and discerning how we may support them in responding to AIDS on the front lines.

Conclusion

Given that HIV/AIDS is most acute among the poor, the impoverished and the marginalized, and that it is spreading most rapidly among women, leaving millions of children orphaned around the world, this pandemic is an urgent occasion for Christians to practice "pure and undefiled religion" (James 1:27). Because we recognize that brokenness fractures all facets of human life, including the physical, spiritual, psychological and social, we seek to stand with those whose bodies and spirits have been devastated by disease and suffering, focusing not only on the pandemic itself but also on the issues that exacerbate it.

In all of our efforts, as God's people we proclaim the life, death, and resurrection of Jesus Christ. We affirm that, in the end, true and lasting healing is found only in a living embrace of the Gospel. Given that personal and social transformation is the work of God, we offer ourselves to God, in full confidence that He will sanctify our efforts to His good purposes. In all of this we endeavor to glorify God as we seek to fulfill our Christian responsibilities through prayer and action "for Christ and His Kingdom."

Eastern Mennonite Missions[5]

Ministering to Those Affected by HIV/AIDS

While the Bible does not mention HIV and AIDS specifically, we can draw on a number of biblical principles that help us to identify our role as Christians in working with people with HIV and AIDS.

Principle 1: HIV Is a Consequence of Universal Sin,
Not God's Punishment on Individuals

One of the biggest barriers to churches working with people with HIV and AIDS is the incorrect belief that HIV is a punishment from God for the way they live their lives. When HIV started to spread rapidly in the 1980s, it spread mainly among certain groups of people that included men who have sexual intercourse with men, commercial sex workers, and people who inject drugs. This has often led to the view that HIV is a punishment from God on individuals. However, HIV affects us all in some way, and, to some extent, we are all at risk of contracting HIV.

In Genesis 3, Adam and Eve decided they wanted to live their lives their own way and turned their backs on God. This meant that human relationships with God, self, others, and creation were damaged. The consequences of sin include suffering, disease, poverty, and exploitation.

We are all vulnerable to HIV infection because we live in a fallen society. For example, poverty may push people into practices that put them at greater risk of infection. Conflict may increase the likelihood of contracting HIV through rape or blood transfusions. Women's low status in some societies may lead them to being sexually exploited.

For many years, HIV and AIDS were seen as the problem of people outside the Church. However, churches now have to accept that HIV and AIDS are present among church members. As more and more people are dying from AIDS, it is becoming a subject that communities are talking about more openly. This may make it easier for church members to be open about their HIV status.

5. Online: www.emm.org/get-involved/give/AIDSManualFinalized.pdf.

Principle 2: God Has Set Boundaries to Help Protect Us and Enable Us to Live Lives Honoring to Him

Much HIV transmission in the world occurs as a result of sexual intercourse that is outside God's plan. While some people might know that sexual intercourse outside of marriage is against God's values, there are others who are not aware of God's framework for sexual behavior. Often sex is a taboo subject within churches. Church leaders have a role in teaching God's plan for sex.

Principle 3: But He Calls Us to Show Compassion to All

Jesus showed compassion to all he met, and we should do the same. When we know people who have HIV due to sinful practices, such as adultery, it can be tempting to withhold love from them. If they infect their faithful partners with HIV, it is easy to blame them and treat them badly in order to punish them. However, Jesus came to save sinners—like us. We must show grace, love, and compassion to all people with the hope that they will become open to being transformed by Jesus.

Principle 4: We Are Called to Protect the Vulnerable and Challenge Injustice

One aspect of the fallen society in which we live is negative attitudes toward women. For example, a woman might become a commercial sex worker because she has no other choice. This may be because she is discriminated against in the employment sector because she is a woman, or it may be because she did not receive the same level of education as men. While her lifestyle is not what God wants for her, this example shows that society as a whole has a part to play in encouraging the spread of HIV. Empowerment of women may take time, but it could be, at minimum, one effective way of reducing the spread of HIV in the long term.

We also have an essential role in caring for widows and orphans, who are often left behind to fend for themselves when husbands or parents die because of AIDS.

How Churches Can Respond to HIV and AIDS

In many places, churches have been mobilized and have been making a positive contribution to action against the AIDS epidemic. However, churches that want to reach out to people affected by HIV and AIDS in their communities may find that their capacity to do so is being reduced because so many of their own members are becoming sick. This is particularly the case in Sub-Saharan Africa. At the same time, they may find that needs in their communities are increasing as HIV spreads. However, doing something is better than doing nothing. Around the globe, churches should be doing something positive to respond to HIV and AIDS in the light of Jesus's commandment to "love your neighbor as yourself" (Luke 10:27).

Good church leadership is essential. What church leaders say and do can have an important impact on those who attend their churches and on people in the local community. It is beneficial to involve church leaders because:

1. Leaders are recognized by the community

2. Leaders can give powerful encouragement to members of the church

3. Leaders often have links to other churches, organizations, and people in positions of responsibility in the community, as well as links to networks at the national level

4. Since they are responsible for preaching sermons on Sundays, leaders have an important role in teaching about issues related to HIV and AIDS.

However, it can be the church leaders who are least willing to admit that HIV is a problem in their communities. They may be fearful that talking about HIV and AIDS may harm their reputation due to stigma. They may not believe that their church should be reaching out to their community in practical ways. Members who are convinced that their church should be taking action in their communities should first talk to the church leadership. It might be necessary for them to raise awareness and educate the church leaders about HIV and AIDS issues so that they can make informed decisions about whether to mobilize the church. If the leaders then show no interest, their blessing should be sought for the work, even if they do not want to actively participate.

There are many ways in which churches can reach out to their communities:

1. Educate people about HIV—about its existence, how it spreads, how to reduce risk of infection, and how to care for people with HIV and AIDS and the affected community

2. Offer hope in Jesus for those living with HIV and AIDS

3. Offer support and love to those living with and those affected by HIV and AIDS

4. Offer practical help to households that have sick members

5. Promote reconciliation among community and family members who struggle to ask for, or to provide, forgiveness for ungodly behavior that has led to infection with HIV

6. Ensure that those living with HIV and AIDS are welcome to attend church and community activities

7. Ensure that orphans are cared for

8. Take steps to reduce stigma and discrimination

9. Advocate for the rights of people living with HIV and AIDS

10. Challenge cultural norms that are harmful to the status of women

11. Provide training on building strong and loving relationships.

How Christian Development Organizations Can Respond to HIV and AIDS

There are many different responses that Christian organizations can make to the HIV/AIDS pandemic. If at all possible, rather than having a large nonprofit "take over," it is best to enable local churches to respond. By working together and coordinating activities, churches and Christian organizations can have greater impact in the fight against AIDS. There are some types of action that are done best, and most cost-effectively, by members of local churches. For example, churches may be able to provide volunteers to care for people living with HIV and AIDS in their homes. This can be far more beneficial than caring for people in hospital. On the other hand, there are some types of action that are best done by Christian organizations, which local churches can refer people to. For example, organizations could provide health care or professional counseling and HIV testing services.

The Faith-Based Perspective on AIDS

Danny McCain, Associate Professor, Department of Religious Studies, University of Jos, Nigeria.[6]

Introduction

There are two things that are growing in Nigeria. The first is religion. This is illustrated by two statements that I frequently hear: "There is a church on every corner in Nigeria, and in every school in between." (Not only are all the traditional churches growing; there are many new, smaller, independent churches springing up everywhere.) "There is no more sleeping in any Nigerian city again after 5:00 AM." This is because there are so many new mosques being built. These two "complaints" describe the condition of religion in Nigeria at the present time. Both Christianity and Islam are alive and well in Nigeria. Both religions are practiced widely. Both religions have high visibility. Both religions are having a major impact in the lives of their adherents. The faith communities are an integral part of the Nigerian society. Remove religion from the society, and the society would be empty and dead.

The second thing that is growing is HIV/AIDS. It is not necessary in this forum to detail the staggering statistics of the rapid and deadly growth of HIV that leads to AIDS in Africa and Nigeria specifically. It is sufficient to point out that many experts are saying that AIDS is the single biggest crisis to ever touch the African continent.

The questions are: Are these two phenomena related in any way? Does one influence the other? Does one have any bearing on the other? Does one have the ability to restrict the advance of the other? I think the answer to those questions is an unqualified "yes."

AIDS is affecting the religious community in several ways. First, many, if not most, of the people suffering from AIDS are religious people. They are people who are members of churches and mosques. Anything that affects the people of any religion affects the religion itself. Second, resources that would normally go to enhancing and promoting the religion are now being diverted to care for people suffering from AIDS. This includes financial resources as well as human resources. Building projects that religious organizations would like to construct and activities that need to be developed

6. Online: http://www.iics.com/aboutus/leadership/mccain/.

have been postponed or cancelled due to lack of funds. People who used to devote time to religious and charitable causes are now involved in caring for people suffering from AIDS.

Third, AIDS is even touching the lives of religious leaders. In the last year or so, nearly every seminary in Jos has lost someone in leadership to AIDS. Three years ago, I conducted an AIDS training workshop for teachers in Gombe State. Within four months, two of those 80 teachers had become sick from AIDS. Even religious teachers are not exempt from AIDS.

I believe that the religious community also must also have a serious impact upon the AIDS crisis. The faith community has a significant contribution to make in many areas of the AIDS battle. This is the case that we wish to present.

Africa and the Faith Community

Religion is a universal phenomenon: Recognizing and attempting to worship a Divine Being is an experience shared by all the world's cultures. Though rationalism has undermined some of the religious commitment previously expressed in the Western world, religion is still a very important part of the lives of most people in the world.

Religion Is Very Popular in Africa

Africans have always been religious. When Islam and Christianity came to Africa, they did not meet a religious vacuum. The fervor and commitment to the traditional religions was transferred to these new religions. Religion is practiced very publicly in Africa. Muslims interrupt their daily activities five times a day to pray, and they do so publicly if necessary. Most public gatherings are opened and closed with prayer. African languages have been deeply impacted by religion and are filled with blessings, prayers, and thanksgiving to God. A very large percentage of names in Africa are connected with God. It is generally assumed in Africa that everyone will be committed to a religion and will practice that religion.

Religion Is One of the Highest Motivations in Life

Because religion deals with one's perception of the creator and owner of the universe, most people take their religion seriously. People will do the most extreme things in the name of religion. Religious adherents invest much time in their fulfilling their religious responsibilities, often many hours a week. Even poor people give large percentages of their money in the name of their religion. Others make long, dangerous, and expensive pilgrimages in the name of religion. Some even refuse to marry and live celibate lives in the name of religion. At times, in order to obey the dictates of their religion, people give up food and other pleasures for long periods of time in the name of religion. People often dress in ways that are contrary to the cultural accepted standards in the name of their religion.

Once people are convinced that their religion demands a certain practice, they are normally willing to fulfill that practice, regardless of the cost, suffering, or stigma that might be associated with that. Therefore, if individuals can be convinced that they are doing a thing in the name of their religion, then there is a much higher likelihood that that particular thing will be done.

AIDS and the Faith Community

How does the faith community specifically impact the issue of AIDS? Religion teaches morality.

The foundation of morality is religion. To say this another way, a culture gets its understanding of right and wrong primarily from its religion. Even the person who claims to practice no religion recognizes that religious beliefs and practices provide stability, order, and justice in society. One of the areas of morality that adherents of Christianity and Islam feel especially strong about is the issue of sexual morality. One of the Ten Commandments says, "You shall not commit adultery" (Exodus 20:14). The Qur'an says, "Nor come nigh to adultery; for it is an indecent (deed) and an evil way" (Al-Israi, Q. 17:32). In fact, both of the sacred books are filled with examples and instructions about proper sexuality.

Once a person becomes infected, there is a high likelihood that he or she is going to pass the infection along to his or her marriage partner. Except for a contaminated blood transfusion, an occasional medical accident, or another rare means of acquiring the infection, most of the time

HIV enters the marriage because one of the partners was infected through sex before marriage or sex outside of marriage. Both of these practices are considered immoral by Christians and Muslims.

Practicing Religious Principles Related to Sex Is the Best Way to Avoid HIV

If a person does not have sex before marriage and remains faithful to his or her marriage partner all throughout the marriage—and the marriage partner does the same—there is very little chance that that person is going to be infected with HIV through sex. Therefore, teaching and encouraging people to practice religious principles related to sex will greatly assist in preventing the spread of HIV. Since one of the highest motivations in life is religion, and since the two major religions in Nigeria agree on sexual abstinence before marriage and faithfulness within marriage, and since observing those practices would stop a large portion of HIV infection, then the two major religions must assume an important role in the AIDS battle in Nigeria. In fact, it would be extremely irresponsible for religious leaders to ignore their responsibility to the HIV/AIDS crisis. It is also irresponsible for government and other agencies involved in AIDS work to ignore the major contribution that religious leaders and religious teachings make in this struggle.

Prevention

Since the message of the church and of the mosque is the best message for stopping the spread of HIV, the leaders of these faith communities must be very involved in prevention. This has already been addressed above; however, I will make an additional observation: Talking about things related to sex has traditionally been considered taboo in many African cultures and many other parts of the world. Sex is something practiced in private. We do not feel comfortable talking about it. However, the fact of the matter is that the Christian and Muslim leaders no longer have the luxury of not talking about sex. The issue must be discussed very openly in the church and in the mosque.

The Bible and the Qur'an both talk about sex. Rather than being embarrassed about this subject and viewing the discussion of sex as a negative thing, religious leaders should be anticipatory and strategic in use of the opportunities that these texts give them. The secular world has had the advantage in talking about sex, and they have done so very freely. Their message is that "everyone does it" whether they are married or not. They have promoted the belief that sex is good anytime, with anyone, for any reason. In response to this secular message, the faith community has basically been negative. Our message has been, "This is bad. Don't get involved in sexual activity." Unfortunately, we have not often provided a positive alternative.

The AIDS crisis, however, is giving to the faith community the opportunity to talk about sex in a positive and wholesome manner, as God intended. The Bible says that when God looked out over all that he had made, including human sexuality, he said, "It is all very good" (Genesis 1:31). Christian and Muslim leaders must take the initiative and make sure that we are presenting a positive and wholesome message about human sexuality. The AIDS crisis gives the religious community the opportunity of addressing issues that we have largely been silent about. It gives us the opportunity to teach our young girls that it is appropriate to resist the sexual advances of older men. It gives us the chance to encourage those men to repent and come into a right relationship with God and with other people. It gives us the opportunity to correct many misunderstandings about sex even among married people.

Therefore, religious leaders must work hard at developing strategies, programs, materials, and personnel to encourage the people under their spiritual care to live according to God's standards for sex. This will help to slow down the steady progress of AIDS.

Care

The faith community must address the issues related to people living with AIDS. One of these issues is removing the stigma associated with AIDS. Whether we like to admit it or not, the faith community holds some of the responsibility for the way that society views people living with HIV/AIDS. In the early days of this crisis, AIDS was viewed as a homosexual disease, and, in some sense, a judgment by God for perverted behavior. This perception has not been found in Africa so much because AIDS, even in the early days, was part of the heterosexual community. Therefore, in Africa, AIDS was viewed as God's judgment upon people for fornication or adultery. Whereas there are often consequences to ignoring God's standards, people of faith, and especially the leaders of the Christian and

Muslim communities, must take the lead in helping to remove the stigma associated with HIV/AIDS.

AIDS is often linked with two things in the New Testament. AIDS is viewed today much as leprosy was in biblical days. What, though, was Jesus's attitude toward leprosy? When Jesus met a leper, he reached out his hand and touched him, doing something almost no one in that society would have ever done. This is a remarkable example of the way we should respond to people living with HIV/AIDS. People of faith must have compassion toward those living with HIV/AIDS and must demonstrate it in a personal way.

AIDS is also often linked with immorality. When it becomes known that a person is HIV-positive, often those who learn about it assume that the person contracted the infection through fornication or adultery. Even if this is true, Jesus gives us a remarkable example of the way we should respond to people who have been guilty of immorality. The Pharisees caught a woman once in the very act of adultery and brought her to Jesus. Her accusers wanted to use her to trap Jesus. However, Jesus's message to her was very simple: He said to her, "Go now and leave your life of sin" (John 8:11). Jesus had an attitude of forgiveness and compassion.

We, as people of faith, should never do or teach anything that would encourage people to become sexually immoral. Forgiveness does not necessarily mean removal of the consequences of our actions. However, once a person has become guilty of immorality, even if that has manifested itself in becoming HIV-positive, people of faith must offer those persons the forgiveness of God. We must leave condemnation and judgment up to God. We must reject and correct the idea that, because this person has sinned, he or she is not worthy of our human love, support, and forgiveness. We must be in the forefront of removing the stigma from people who are already suffering enough from HIV/AIDS.

HIV/AIDS has created the need for new and better counseling techniques. One of the greatest blessings of life is not knowing when we will die. If we knew that we were going to die next week, it would be difficult to enjoy life today. Unfortunately, people living with HIV/AIDS, as with other terminally ill patients, live with the realization that there is an outside limit to the length of their lives. This reality creates additional stresses that ordinary people do not have to deal with. In addition, the families of people living with HIV/AIDS often need counseling because the grief over losing their loved ones begins before the person dies. Certainly, after a person dies from AIDS, the family not only needs typical counseling support that any family would need from losing a loved one; they often need to overcome the stigma that their loved one died from AIDS. In light of this, the community of faith must develop specific strategies for counseling all who are affected by AIDS.

The faith community must provide training in the care of HIV/AIDS patients. There are now so many AIDS patients in Nigeria that the hospitals and clinics cannot take care of them. Most hospitals now send AIDS patients home to die. This situation is likely to get much worse before it gets better. Therefore, in the near future, it will be the responsibility of family members and close friends to take care of AIDS patients until they die. One of the most practical benefits of most major religions has been the creation of procedures, policies, and agencies for taking care of the needy. The mosque and church have always been places of compassion. This characteristic of organized religions will be stretched to its limit with the AIDS crisis.

Both Christianity and Islam teach the importance of caring for the needy. Therefore, people of faith will need to create programs, agencies, and facilities to teach their people how to care for those suffering from AIDS. They need to do this in such a way as to provide the maximum amount of comfort and love to family members while at the same time protecting themselves and other family members from contracting HIV.

Orphans

AIDS strikes people during their most sexually active years. Those years are when young adults are producing and raising children. The largest number of AIDS victims is in the age bracket of 20 to 40. When a man dies from AIDS, it is likely that he has infected his wife, or vice versa. Both eventually die, leaving the children behind. Because of this pattern, there may be as many as 30 million children newly orphaned due to AIDS in the next 10 years. This is obviously an unbelievable problem. I read about one grandmother in Uganda who is taking care of 38 grandchildren. She had six children, and all of her children and all of their spouses contracted AIDS and died. If there are no grandparents or other adults to take care of orphans, then the older children have to take care of the junior ones. Twelve-year-old children are now taking care of many younger brothers and sisters.

The faith community has traditionally been concerned about orphans. However, orphanages have not been as common in Africa because of the very strong extended family network. But when the extended family is destroyed because so many young adults are dying, the church or the mosque is going to have to step in and take care of these innocent victims of AIDS. People of faith have always taken care of the vulnerable people in society. Therefore, communities of faith must do whatever is necessary to take care of the thousands of children being orphaned every day because of this crisis.

Faith Responses to AIDS in Public Schools

One of the good things about Nigeria is that, unlike in some of the Western nations, there is no attempt to separate religion from public life. In fact, one of the most positive characteristics of the educational system is that religion is taught and encouraged in the public schools. Because of this, the public schools are one the most strategic places for fighting the AIDS battle using faith-based approaches.

Conclusion

AIDS is killing us in Africa. For reasons we do not fully understand, however, God Almighty has chosen our particular generation to fight this battle. This is not a battle that one person or one part of society can fight alone. We cannot leave the battle against AIDS up to medical people only. It will take the combined efforts of all of us—the medical community, the business community, the educational community, and certainly the religious community—to fight and win this battle. God is on our side. We believe that we will someday prevail.

APPENDIX 3

Glossary[1]

A

Advocacy and support groups. Organizations and groups that actively support participants and their families with valuable resources, including self-empowerment and survival tools.

Antibody. An infection-fighting protein molecule in blood or body fluid that tags, neutralizes, and helps destroy bacteria, viruses, or other harmful toxins. Antibodies, known generally as immunoglobulins, are made by white blood cells in response to a foreign substance. Each specific antibody binds only to the specific antigen that stimulated its production.

Antiretroviral (ARV). The human immunodeficiency virus (HIV) belongs to a class of viruses that are called retroviruses. Drugs that control the growth of the virus are called antiretrovirals.

Approved drugs. In the United States, the Food and Drug Administration (FDA) must approve a substance as a drug before it can be marketed. The approval process involves several steps, including pre-clinical laboratory and animal studies, clinical trials for safety and efficacy, filing of a New Drug Application by the manufacturer of the drug, FDA review of the application, and FDA approval/rejection of the application (See Food and Drug Administration).

ART (Antiretroviral treatment). Formally known as HAART (Highly Active Antiretroviral Treatment), ART is treatment with at least three active antiretroviral medications (ARVs) and typically two nucleoside or nucleotide reverse transcriptase inhibitors (NRTIs), plus a non-nucleoside

---

1. Modified from Center for HIV Information, University of California, and Center for AIDS Research, NYU School of Medicine.

reverse transcriptase inhibitor (NNRTI) or a protease inhibitor (PI). ART is often called the drug "cocktail" or triple-therapy.

B

Bactrim. An antibiotic that is used to treat common bacterial infections, such as ear and intestinal infections and pneumonia. It also has some activity against malaria. It is used prophylactically to prevent opportunistic infections in patients with HIV. Also known as cotrimoxazole, trimethoprim-sulfamethoxazole, and Septrin.

C

CBO (community-based organization). A group of individuals or independent groups that forms an organization to address issues within their community.

CD4 cell counts. A CD4 cell is a white blood cell that mobilizes the immune defense when the body has an infection. A CD4 cell count is a measure of the immune system's health. HIV specifically attacks and destroys CD4 cells, and most patients infected with HIV have low CD4 cell counts.

Clinical. Pertaining to or founded on observation and treatment of participants, as distinguished from theoretical or basic science.

Combination therapy. Two or more antiretroviral drugs or treatments used together to achieve optimum results against HIV infection and/or AIDS. Combining drugs has proved to be more effective at reducing the amount of the HIV in the body than the use of single drugs by themselves.

Complete blood count (CBC). A measure of the health of the blood, including the quality and quantity of its white and red blood cells. The CBC includes 13 tests. The three main tests are the white blood cell count (WBC), hemoglobin (HGB), and platelets.

Confidentiality. Refers to maintaining the privacy of patients with HIV to avoid discrimination and stigmatization.

Cotrimoxazole. See Bactrim.

D

Developing country. See Resource-poor country.

Drug resistance. Occurs when the virus a person is infected with is no longer sensitive to the medications taken.

E

Efficacy (of a drug or treatment). The maximum ability of a drug or treatment to produce a result regardless of dosage.

ELISA (enzyme-linked immunoabsorbent assay). A blood test that detects antibodies based on a reaction that leads to a color change in the test tube. The HIV ELISA is commonly used as the initial screening test because it is relatively easy and inexpensive to perform. A positive HIV ELISA test must be confirmed by a second, more specific test, such as a Western Blot.

Epidemiology. The branch of medical science that deals with the study of incidence, distribution, and control of a disease in a population.

F

Faith-based organization (FBO). A single religious group or multiple religious groups, including denominations, inclusive of all religions, that provide service and care.

FDA. See Food and Drug Administration.

Food and Drug Administration (FDA). The U.S. Department of Health and Human Services agency responsible for ensuring the safety and effectiveness of all drugs, biologics, vaccines, and medical devices, including those used in the diagnosis, treatment, and prevention of HIV infection, AIDS, and AIDS-related opportunistic infections.

G

Gender-based violence. WHO defines gender-based violence (GBV) as any act of violence that results in, or is likely to result in, physical, sexual, or psychological harm or suffering to women (or men), including threats of such acts, coercion, or arbitrary deprivations of liberty, whether occurring in public or in private life. Many authors refer to violence against an individual in an intimate partner relationship as intimate partner violence (IPV). See also intimate partner violence.

Growth and development. The growth in weight, height, and psychosocial and neurological development that occurs with age.

H

HAART (Highly Active Antiretroviral Treatment). Administration of at least three active antiretroviral medications (ARVs). HAART is often called the drug "cocktail" or triple-therapy (See also ART).

Health care worker. An individual who cares for patients; includes doctors, nurses, and nurse practitioners.

Human immunodeficiency virus type 1 (HIV-1). The retrovirus isolated and recognized as the cause of AIDS. HIV-1 is classified as a lentivirus in a subgroup of retroviruses. The genetic material of a retrovirus such as HIV is the RNA itself. HIV converts its RNA into DNA and inserts into the host cell's DNA, preventing the host cell from carrying out its natural functions and turning it into an HIV factory.

Human immunodeficiency virus type 2 (HIV-2). A virus closely related to HIV-1 that has also been found to cause AIDS. It was first isolated in West Africa. Although HIV-1 and HIV-2 are similar in their viral structure, modes of transmission, and disease manifestation, HIV-2 is less aggressive than HIV-1 and does not always react to HIV medications in the same way as HIV-1.

I

Immune deficiency. A breakdown or inability of certain parts of the immune system to function, thus making a person susceptible to opportunistic infections, or diseases that they would not ordinarily develop. Also known as immunodeficiency.

Immunity. Natural or acquired resistance provided by the immune system to a specific disease or toxin. Immunity may be partial or complete, specific or nonspecific, long-lasting or temporary.

Immunization. The process of inducing immunity by administering an antigen (vaccine) that is derived from or similar to the infectious agent, in order to allow the immune system to prevent infection or illness when it subsequently encounters the infectious agent.

Informed consent. The process of learning the key facts before intervening in care and treatment or in clinical trials. It is a continuing process to provide information to patients and children and their caregivers.

Intimate partner violence (IPV). The term intimate partner violence (IPV) describes physical, sexual, or psychological harm by a current or former partner or spouse. This type of violence can occur among heterosexual or same-sex couples and does not require sexual intimacy. See also gender-based violence.

J, K, L

Lymphocyte. A type of white blood cell produced in the lymphoid organs that are primarily responsible for immune responses. Lymophocytes are present in the blood, lymph, and lymphoid tissues.

M, N

Non-government organization (NGO). A group or multiple groups that form a non–government-related organization to meet specific needs in a community or country. An NGO usually obtains official government recognition and approval, although this may not be the case in all countries. Funding often comes from foundations and international organizations.

Nucleoside reverse transcriptase inhibitor (NRTI). A nucleoside analog antiretroviral drug whose chemical structure is made up of a modified version of a natural nucleoside. These compounds suppress reproduction of retroviruses by interfering with the reverse transcriptase enzyme. Examples include zidovudine, lamivudine, and stavudine.

O

Opportunistic infection. An illness caused by an organism that usually does not cause disease in a person with a normal immune system. People with advanced HIV infection suffer from opportunistic infections of the lungs, brain, eyes, and other organs.

Orphans and vulnerable children (OVC). For purposes of the HIV epidemic, the World Health Organization defines an orphan as a child younger than 18 years of age who has lost one or both parents to HIV/AIDS. Children who have lost one parent are considered orphans because the remaining parent is often too ill to work or support the family. The terms orphan and vulnerable child are both used to describe these children; includes both those who are infected with HIV and those who are uninfected.

P

PCR (polymerase chain reaction). A sensitive laboratory technique used to detect the amount of HIV RNA in the blood. PCR is used to measure viral load (amount of virus) in persons infected with HIV. PCR measures the amount of the virus itself in contrast to amount of antibodies, which measures the immune response to the virus.

PEPFAR ([U.S.] President's Emergency Plan for AIDS Relief). A budget of $15 billion approved by Congress to provide for worldwide HIV programs that address treatment, prevention, and orphan and palliative care. Limited to certain countries.

PEP (post-exposure prophylaxis). Use of drugs to prevent an infection after exposure to the infecting agent. In relation to HIV, use of antiretroviral drugs following accidental inoculation of blood or other body fluids from a patient with HIV or following rape.

Perinatal. Before and after delivery of an infant.

PMTCT (Prevention of mother–to-child transmission of HIV). Usually achieved by use of HAART and formula feeding rather than breast-feeding.

Prenatal. Before delivery of an infant.

Primary care provider. A health care professional who provides medical care. Can be a medical doctor or physician (MD), a physician's assistant (PA), or a nurse practitioner (NP). Primary care providers conduct regular physical exams and take care of patients' health care needs.

Prophylaxis. Prevention of infection.

Protease inhibitor. One of a class of anti-HIV drugs designed to inhibit the enzyme protease and interfere with virus replication. Protease inhibitors prevent HIV precursor proteins from dividing into smaller cells of active proteins, a process that normally occurs when HIV reproduces.

Q

Quality of life. The everyday feeling or documented quality of living. Measure includes ability to work, think, walk, etc.

R

Rapid HIV test. A simplified and inexpensive antibody test for HIV that is used primarily in resource-poor countries. Test results are available on the same day that the test is performed. Not useful for testing infants until they have reached 12 to 18 months of age and until breast-feeding has ceased for at least three months.

Resource-poor country. A country with inadequate resources to meet normally accepted needs such as health care, education, water, and food. Also known as a developing country.

Retrovirus. HIV and other viruses that carry their genetic material in the form of RNA rather than DNA and have the enzyme, reverse transcriptase, that can transcribe the RNA into DNA. In most animals and plants, DNA is usually made into RNA; hence "retro" is used to indicate the opposite direction.

Reverse transcriptase. The enzyme produced by HIV and other retroviruses that enable them to direct a cell to synthesize DNA from their viral RNA.

S

Standard treatment. A health protocol, currently in wide use and approved by the FDA, considered to be effective in the care of a patient with a specific disease or condition.

Standards of care. Treatment regimen or medical management based on state-of-the-art care recommended by experts. National Ministries of Health often develop guidelines for standards of care for various diseases.

T

Toxicity. An adverse effect produced by a drug that is detrimental to the participant's health. The level of toxicity associated with a drug will vary depending on the condition that the drug is used to treat.

U, V

Vaccine. A preparation that, when injected into the body, stimulates an immune response that can prevent an infection or create resistance to an infection. Some vaccines, such as polio, are given by mouth. The infectious agent in the vaccine may be either killed or attenuated.

Viral load. Measurement of the amount of new HIV produced and released into a person's bloodstream.

Virus. A microorganism composed of a piece of genetic material, RNA or DNA, covered by a protein coat. To replicate itself, a virus must infect a cell and direct the cellular machinery to produce new viruses.

W, X, Y, Z

Western Blot. A blood test used to detect antibodies to several specific components of a virus such as HIV. This test is most often used to confirm a positive ELISA test.

Window period. Amount of time between exposure to HIV and development of antibodies. If you take an HIV test during the window period, the result may not be a true reflection of your HIV status.

WHO (World Health Organization). Worldwide organization responsible for developing consensus guidelines for international public health.